AF579072

Projects in Tatting

Projects in Tatting

SHEILA YORK

Dryad Press Ltd, London

Dedicated to the workers of the past who kept the craft of Tatting alive for me to enjoy.

ISBN 0 8521 9594 X

Typeset by Servis Filmsetting Ltd, Manchester

Printed in Great Britain
by Anchor Brendon Ltd
Tiptree, Essex
for the publishers
Dryad Press Ltd
4 Fitzhardinge Street
London W1H 0AH

Contents

Acknowledgment

Particular thanks are due to the following who have helped me in preparing the work for this book: my family who have been called upon regularly (and have usually agreed) to admire or discuss some weird and wonderful prototypes; my husband John who has had to revive a waning interest in photography in order to produce the pictures; my daughters, Louise for acting as a model and Simona for her encouragement and help with the diagrams; my students at the N.E. Hants Institute who have so willingly worked and tested my patterns over the years, and in particular Marilyn Martin and Joan Vernon who, by their enthusiasm for something different, have helped develop my style of tatting.

The pattern for the Pearl Centre Brooch was first published in *Lace*, and the Summer Corner picture was printed in card form by the Lace Guild.

Introduction

I love to tat. Of all the crafts I have really enjoyed, tatting is the one which satisfies me most. I always wanted to tat but I have no idea what it was that I saw or heard which so intrigued me and made me search for years for someone to teach me. Surely the interest cannot have come from literature where tatting is mentioned rather disparagingly, and equally it cannot have been from seeing tatted work around because I have found very little from days gone by. Maybe it was a shuttle; perhaps as a child I played with my grandmother's wooden shuttle which was rediscovered in an old workbox just a few years ago. I should like to think this was the way the seed was sown because tatting has given me so much pleasure which I hope I can now share with others through this book.

It is difficult to identify what it is about tatting that is so fascinating. The simplicity of the stitches and the ease with which tatting may be worked is one obvious attraction, but the fact that so many people find it difficult to master at first but nevertheless persevere suggests that there is something more to tatting. Obviously one incentive to continue is the desire to produce a piece of tatted lace; we like the delicate look of tatting and find the neatness and regularity of the work pleasing to the eye. But the actual working of the tatting has its own satisfaction. The movement of the shuttle is soothing and for such delicate-looking work it is quick to produce. Very little preparation is needed – only the shuttle need be wound with thread. The work can be done almost anywhere, can be picked up and put down at any time, and when the basic stitch is mastered it is easier on the eyes than most fine work.

Some people would accept all these positive comments about tatting but then dismiss the craft with a remark similar to the one which was made to me, 'But you can't do anything with tatting except put it round handkerchiefs and traycloths and I never use either.' Since I was quite a new tatter at the time, happy with my neatly completed hankie edgings and little mats, this remark did not encourage further conversation. It did, however, make me think and provided the stimulus I needed. I began looking at things with new eyes to see how I could introduce tatting effectively into today's way of life. Because tatting had released and fulfilled a creative need in me, I was determined that it was not going to be discarded along with the handkerchiefs and traycloths if I could help it.

I was encouraged in this approach by my first class of students who did not want to work a new handkerchief edging every week but I knew they did not have the expertise to make larger items such as doilies and collars satisfactorily. I scoured books for patterns to adapt for today's use but quickly discovered that there were few patterns, other than edgings, which were simple enough for a beginner to work with confidence. I remembered my own frustration when working my first mat and I then realized that I had not been stupid, the pattern was just too difficult for a beginner. So I found myself having to design, not just anything that took my interest but a series of patterns which would, step by step, teach new workers all the basic tatting techniques. In addition the patterns had to be for a variety of small items which would interest the students and build up their experience and confidence. And so my basic course in tatting evolved and it is given in the section on techniques and in the first nine projects of this book. Beginners are recommended to work right through the course. Those with more experience will find the patterns and ideas useful and may find it interesting to compare their methods of construction with those which I have found effective.

During my first year of teaching I discovered beaded tatting and, being enthralled by its possibilities, I introduced it to the students. I was delighted with their response which meant that more patterns needed to be designed, this time covering the techniques of beaded tatting and working with sequins. A selection of those patterns and some information on beads is given immediately after the basic course since using beads in tatting continues to be so popular. Beads are included in several of the more advanced designs, particularly in the items comprising the jewellery section of the book.

There is still a need for patterns for the home and for gifts and I have included several items in this category in the book. Each pattern in this section has been designed for a specific use to avoid the frustration of producing, for example, a motif which is either too big or too small for any available box or paperweight, but obviously these patterns can also be used in other ways.

The pieces in the final section of the book have a special place in my affections. They were inspired by the beauty of nature, each piece representing one of the four seasons of the year. They introduce some unorthodox ways of tatting in the attempt to capture some of the magic of spring flowers, summer butterflies, autumn mornings and Christmas time.

Throughout the book the patterns are written out in full as is normal in Britain, but they are also broken down into sections with explanatory notes so that the construction of the work is more easily understood. Additionally each pattern has either a diagram or a photograph showing clearly the construction details which workers from other countries will find more familiar. A comprehensive list of suppliers has been assembled and is given to assist workers in obtaining the materials and any accessories necessary for using the patterns in the ways shown.

My hope is that all tatters will enjoy this book and that those who have tatted for some time, together with those who are newer to the craft, will feel stimulated and encouraged to develop their tatting and to use it in different ways for their own pleasure and that of those around them.

1
Tatting Techniques

MATERIALS AND EQUIPMENT FOR TATTING

The word 'tatting' immediately brings to mind the word 'shuttle', but in fact all that is required to produce a piece of tatting is some thread – the hands do the rest. However, it is more convenient to work with the thread wound onto a shuttle.

Shuttles

Shuttles used to be made out of a variety of materials, for example ivory, shell, bone, wood and silver. They were both large and small and some incorporated a hook. Generally the shape and construction were the same, two oval pieces of material riveted on either side of a small block around which the thread was wound.

There are two different types of shuttle readily available on the British market today, both made out of plastic. The Aero shuttle has a removable bobbin for the quick and easy winding of the thread and it has a fine metal hook attached to it for joining the work. The Milward shuttle is more traditionally shaped and has a separate hook for joining. It is a matter of personal opinion which is best. Some workers complain that the shuttle with hook attached is uncomfortable to work with, whereas others will quickly overcome this inconvenience and maintain that to have to drop the shuttle and find the hook for joining interrupts the flow of work. The best shuttle is the one you enjoy working with. Since the shuttle only holds the tatting thread, the same shuttle can be used when working with different thicknesses of thread but of course the shuttle will hold a much longer length of fine thread than thick thread.

It is indicative of the increased interest in tatting that modern handmade shuttles are beginning to become available. There are wooden ones made in the traditional shape in a variety of woods and sometimes decorated, and also silver ones usually made to order from silversmiths. Tatting shuttles are being sold all over the world in different shapes, sizes and colours. Illustration 1 shows a selection from Europe and the United States. Western European countries are mainly reproducing the traditional style in modern materials. In some Eastern European countries they seem to be unobtainable at the present time and workers are encouraged to make their own. The United States of America has the biggest variety of styles, and materials used include wood, plastic and metal. The metal ones have a removable bobbin and a hook attached; some workers like the heavier weight of these but the hook is too thick for joining work with small picots.

Threads

For the majority of tatting, particularly that which will be subjected to wear and will be frequently washed, it is generally recommended that a strong thread with a firm twist

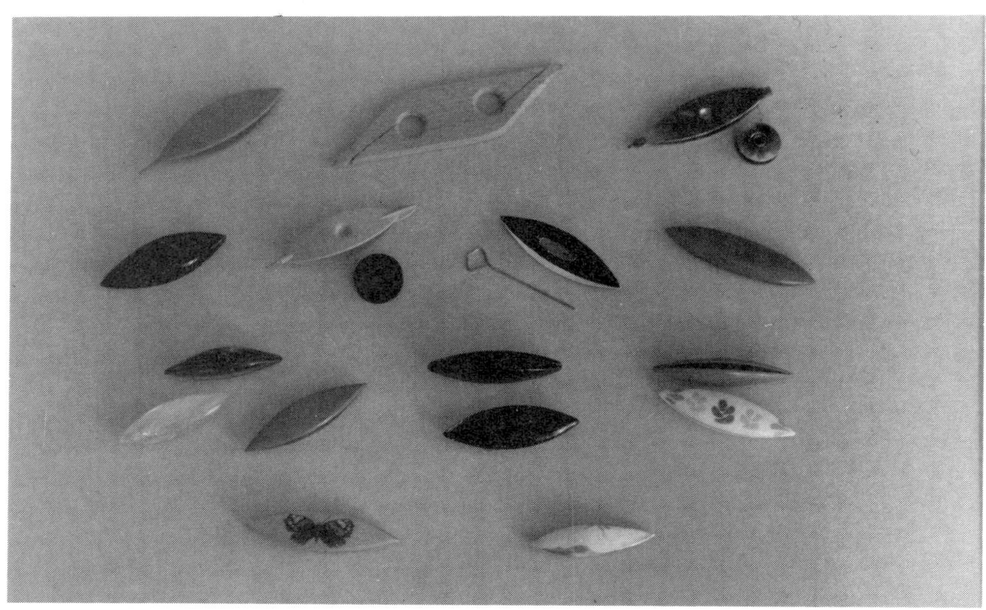

1 A selection of modern shuttles. Left to right: Top row: USA; plastic, wooden, metal; 2nd row: Spanish, British (Aero), British (Milward), Tenerife; 3rd row: 3 Portuguese, 2 Swiss, 2 German; the top 3 shuttles on this row show the widths of the shuttles; 4th row: British painted wooden, British silver

is used. Such threads will hold a firm knot, or stitch, will not fluff or break under normal conditions and will be easy to work with. Crochet cottons in all thicknesses are suitable although some of the thicker threads now available are rather soft. Which thickness, or size, of thread to use will depend on the type of piece to be produced and on the personal preference of the worker. The same tatting pattern can be used to quite different effect simply by changing the size of thread as can be seen in Illustration 2 where the motifs of rings and chains were all made from the same pattern but in different size threads.

It is well worth experimenting with different kinds of threads such as rayon, silk and metallic to see the effects produced. It will be found that one can tat with most threads although some will be more difficult to work with than others – they may break, twist, fray or not produce a firm knot but they may well be useful in a decorative piece of work. It is helpful in planning further work to keep a note and sample of these experiments together with any personal comments. Even with the crochet threads it is worth working a sample motif with notes of the thread used and the construction details since threads produced by different manufacturers work up differently.

THE CONSTRUCTION OF TATTING

Tatting is simple since only one stitch is used, called the double stitch or double knot. This stitch can be made on circles of thread which are then called rings, and on straight lengths of thread which are called chains. Rings and chains can be used on their own but they can also be combined. The work is shaped by regulating the number of stitches in the rings and chains and by joining the work as it progresses. Picots, which are loops of thread, can be made to decorate both the rings and the chains.

2 Sample motifs constructed with the same number of stitches but using different threads. Starting with the smallest motif and working clockwise the threads used were: DMC Broder Machine; Dewhursts Sylko; DMC Cordonnet Special No. 100; DMC Fil a Dentelles; DMC Cordonnet Special No. 60; Coats Mercer Crochet No. 60; Coats Mercer Crochet No. 40; DMC Cordonnet Special No. 30; Coats Mercer Crochet No. 20

3 A series of tatted rings separated by a piece of unworked thread and made with thread from the shuttle

4 A series of rings separated by chains and made with thread from the shuttle and a second thread

5 A series of rings and chains with picots. The rings are joined together to shape the work

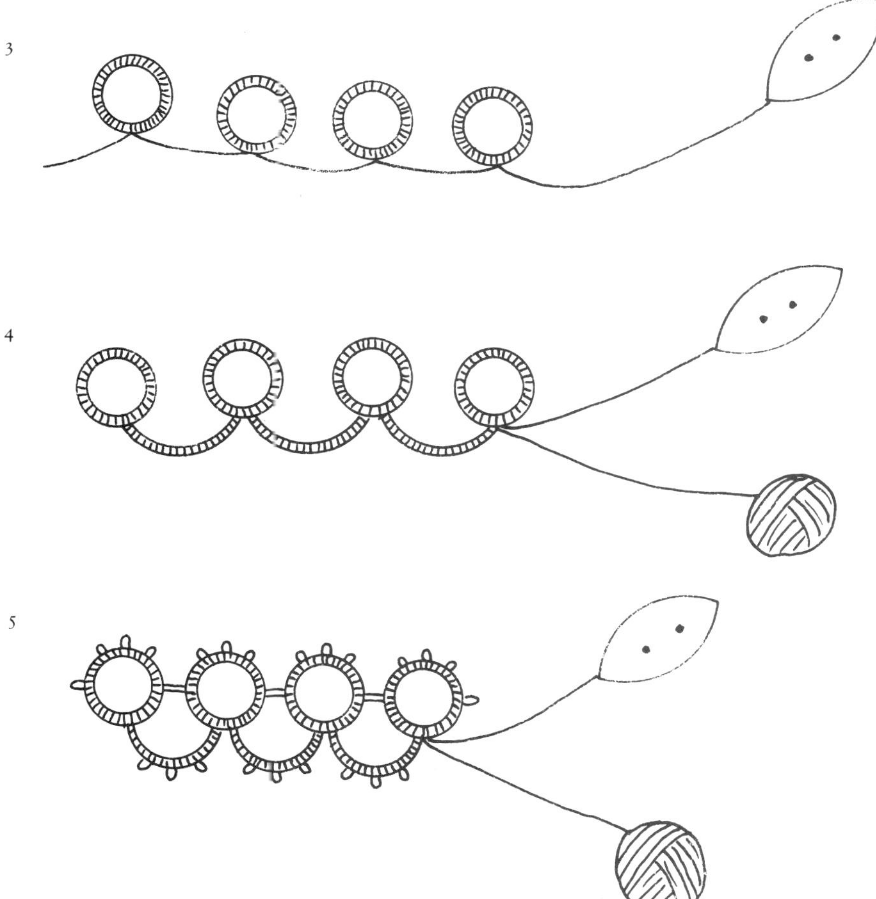

The basic tatting stitch

The double stitch is constructed in two halves, called the first half and the second half. The only complication is that the stitches have to be reversed on the working thread, and it is no comfort to read that it is a knack which is much more easily learnt by watching someone tat than by reading about it! However, the reversing is much simpler to see and to achieve if two threads in different colours are used to construct a chain.

To make the double stitch

Use one dark thread and one light thread of a type such as a No. 10 crochet cotton. Half fill the shuttle with the dark thread, cut it off from the ball and knot the end of the shuttle thread to the end of the light ball of thread. Hold this knot between the thumb and forefinger of the left hand, and obtain some tension on the light thread by taking it across the back of the fore and middle fingers of the left hand and then winding it around the remaining fingers of that hand. *First half stitch:* Release 12in (30cm) of thread from the shuttle, hold the shuttle between the thumb and the first and middle fingers of the right hand with the thread from the shuttle hanging over the palm, and take the thread round and over the back of the right hand. Release the tension of the thread on the left hand and position the hands as shown in Illustration 6. Pass the shuttle under the light thread from *front to back* then over the top of the same thread and down through the loop formed by the shuttle thread on the right hand. * *Keeping the left-hand thread relaxed and still* pull the shuttle thread out to the right and watch the stitch reverse – i.e. the dark thread was 'wound round' the light thread (Illustration 7), but on reversing the light thread ends up 'wound round' the dark thread (Illustration 8). Now *keeping the shuttle thread taut and still* slowly regain the tension on the left hand by lifting the middle finger, and allow the stitch to run down the dark thread and lie close to the knot. *Second half stitch:* Relax the tension of the thread on the left hand. Without winding the shuttle

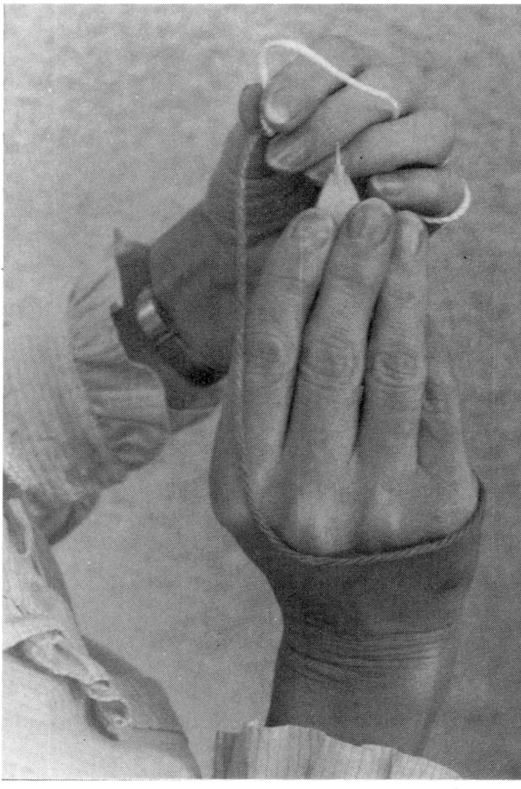

6 The position of the hands and the two threads before making the first half stitch on a chain

7 The unreversed half stitch with the dark thread 'wound round' the light thread

8 The half stitch reversed, the light thread is now 'wound round' the dark thread

9 A series of completed double stitches and showing the position of the working threads

thread around the right hand take the shuttle over the light left-hand thread from *back to front*, and complete the reversing of the stitch by repeating the action of the first half from *. This completes a double stitch.

Note that on this example the double stitch is a light stitch on a dark thread, and check the shape of the stitch with Illustration 9 noting that the shuttle thread leaves the completed stitch at the bottom front and the ball thread at the top back. Continue this

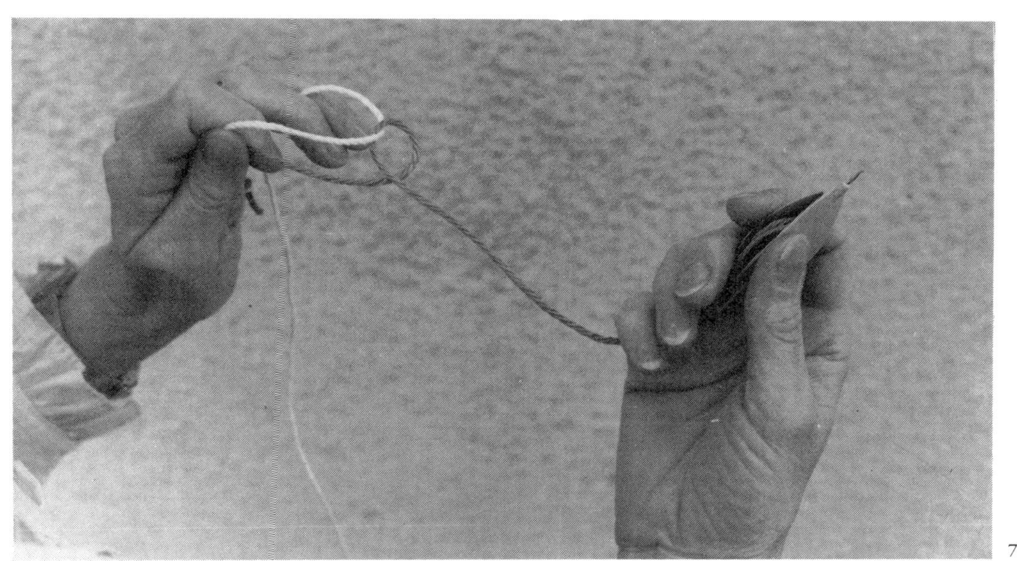
7

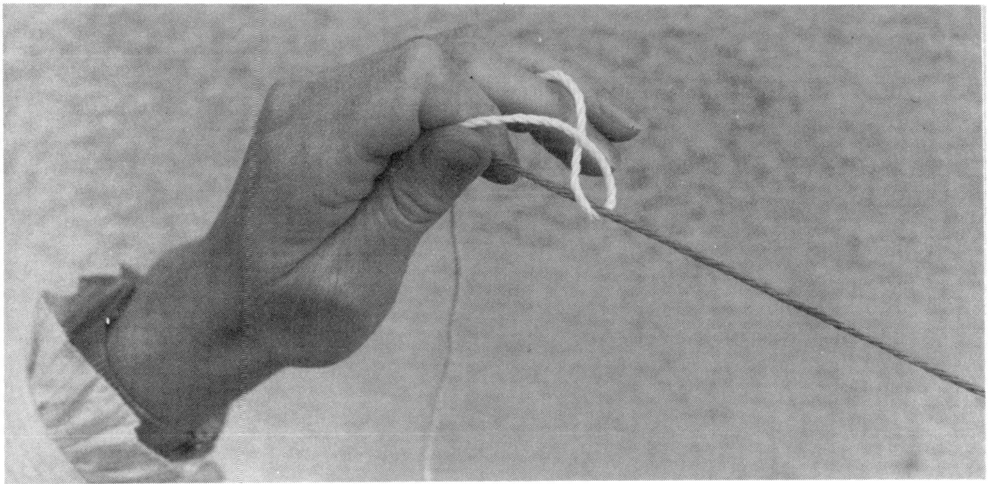
8

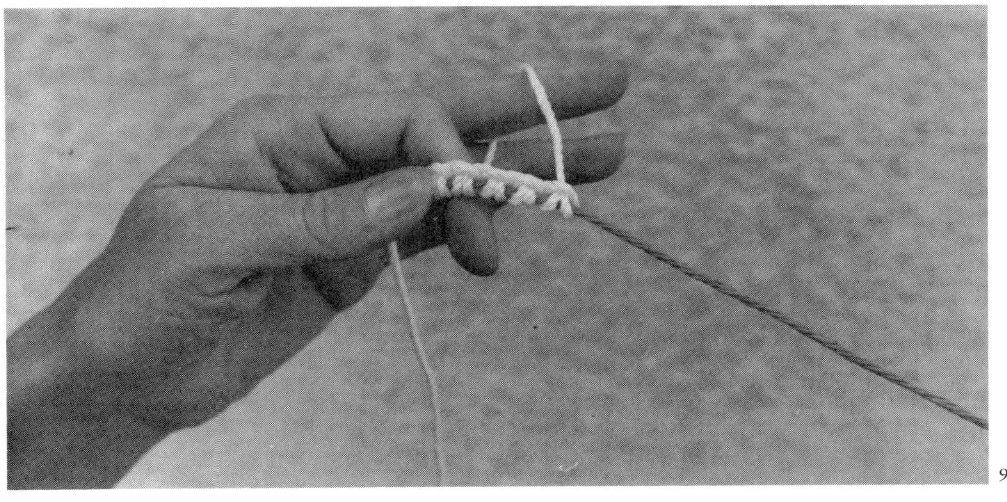
9

process, always making a first half stitch followed by a second half stitch. This series of stitches forms a chain.

Left-handed workers

It will probably be easier to learn the stitch the right-handed way at first. Since the left hand has to work quite hard in tatting they may well find that they can continue to work right-handed, otherwise on understanding the construction procedure all instructions should be reversed.

RINGS AND PICOTS

Rings

When the double stitch is produced without difficulty on the chain few problems arise when moving onto the next stage which is making rings. The same stitch is used but instead of working with two different threads, only the thread from the shuttle is required.

To make a ring

Fill the shuttle with a light-coloured thread and have 12in (30cm) hanging free. Holding the end of the thread between the thumb and forefinger of the left hand, take the shuttle thread round the back of the fingers then across the front of the fingers to the thumb and forefinger, and hold it together with the end of the thread. Then take the shuttle and make a double stitch on the thread which is across the back of the hand in exactly the same way as the stitch was made on the chain. To check that the stitch has reversed, hold the stitch between the thumb and forefinger and gently pull the thread attached to the shuttle – the ring on the hand will become smaller. To enlarge the ring ready for working the next stitch, pull the ring thread which is below the thumb. Make several double stitches on the ring and then close it by pulling the shuttle thread until the stitches at the beginning and end of the ring meet. Leave a small amount of thread and make a further ring in the same way. Try making the next ring as close as possible to the previous one.

Problems with rings

Difficulty may be experienced in closing rings if the stitches are pulled extremely tight, an incorrect stitch has been made or the ring has become damp with perspiration from the hands whilst working. Once rings have been closed it is almost impossible to undo them. If they have been incorrectly made they should be pulled open as much as possible and the opened section cut with scissors. The incorrect ring will then unravel and can be re-worked, but any following rings will have to be re-worked as well.

Picots

These are the loops of thread which can come off rings or chains, and are used for decoration and for joining the tatting during construction. They are formed simply by leaving a gap between the stitches. To practise, make a ring with two double stitches, * form the first half of the next stitch but do not let it slide close to the previous stitch, make the second half of this stitch close to the first half and then push this completed stitch up to the previous stitch. Make one more double stitch as usual then repeat from * until five picots have been made. Close the ring.

Making picots of a regular size comes with practice but for picots of a specific size it is helpful to cut a piece of card with one side twice the width the picot is to be and the other about 3in (7cm) long. This piece of card, often called a spacer, can be placed between the stitches when the picot is being made. See Illustration 10. The size of a picot depends on its use, whether it is to be used for joining or for decoration. Those used for joining must be of such a size that a join can be made easily and the piece of work will lie neatly. The size of decorative picots depends on the preference of the worker and also the use to which the piece of tatting is to be put. Long picots give a delicate look but they can be tedious to keep tidy if the piece is washed

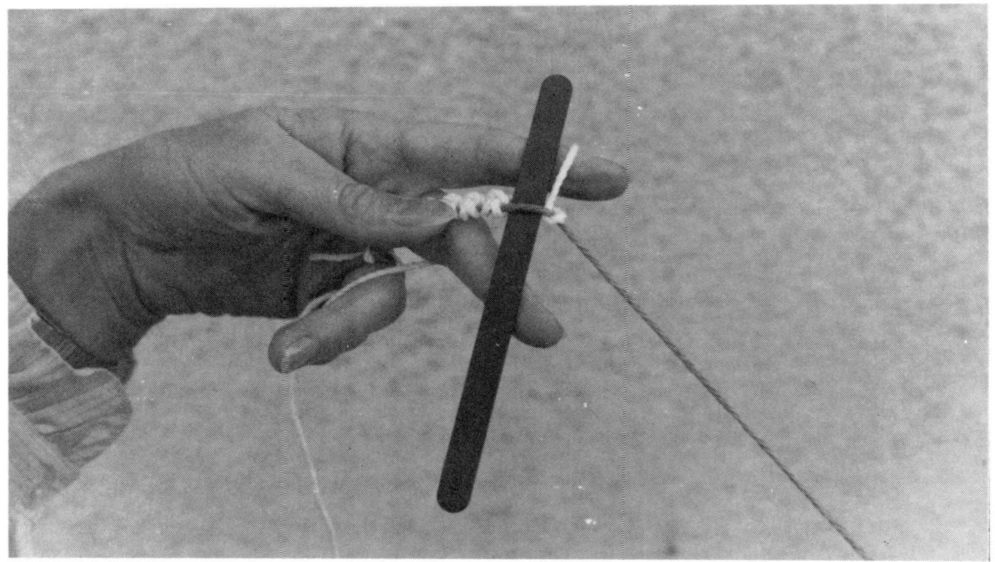

10 A picot being made on a chain with the use of a spacer

frequently. The size, or combination of different sizes, can alter the effect of a pattern quite remarkably and it is well worth spending some time experimenting with different sizes before embarking on a large piece of work.

FINISHING TATTING

The final stage in tatting, finishing the ends and making the piece lie flat and even, is most important in making the tatting look its best. There are different ways of completing both these tasks and which ones are used will depend on the particular piece of work and the preference of the worker.

Finishing ends

Ends to be finished will be found at the beginning and end of the work and also when new threads are joined or a mistake is made. Wherever possible it is best to avoid ends by:

(a) Not cutting the thread at the beginning of a piece of work which requires both ball and shuttle thread, i.e. when both rings and chains are to be made.

(b) Filling the shuttle with sufficient thread to complete the piece of work with as few refills as possible.

(c) Not making mistakes!

Weaving in ends

Often threads can be woven into the tatting as it is being worked and many workers employ this method whenever possible.

To weave a thread into a ring

Start the ring by making the double stitch as usual. Make the first half of the next stitch, but before allowing it to lie close to the first stitch, lay the end thread along the straight shuttle thread and pass the end *down* through the loop formed by the incomplete half stitch. Holding both the shuttle thread and the end taut, allow the half stitch to slide close to the first stitch. Repeat this process with the second half of the stitch but pass the end *up* through the loop formed by the incomplete half stitch. Continue in this way until the end has been worked through three or four stitches, then cut the end off close to the work. This method can be used even when picots occur during the first few stitches.

To weave a thread into a chain

The same process is followed. It is often possible to weave the end of the old shuttle thread into a chain when the shuttle has to be refilled during a piece of work, thereby finishing both old and new ends during the course of the work. Care should be taken to cut the end very close to the work after it has been woven in and also to pull the stitches made over the double thread slightly tighter to disguise the thickness.

Sewing ends down

The very end threads cannot be woven in and so must be finished in another way, usually by being sewn down. Again there are different methods which can be used and it is up to the worker to select the one which will be most effective and as inconspicuous as possible. Whichever method is chosen it is important to use a fine needle so that the shape of the tatting is not distorted. Two different methods are:

(a) The traditional method which is to tie a tight knot and to lay the ends along a ring or chain and to sew them in place with a matching sewing thread.
(b) One which is very similar to the traditional method but instead of using a separate piece of sewing thread the working thread is untwisted and used as follows. Take the end to be sewn down, untwist it and separate out a single strand. Do the same with the second end. Tie a knot with the single strands then lay the remaining strands of one end along a ring or chain, and using the single strand sew it neatly in place. Repeat with the strands of the other end.

Glueing ends down

In some display items, such as paperweights or pictures, the slight thickness of a woven-in end or the stitches of a sewn-down end may be quite noticeable. In these cases and in others such as jewellery where as near invisible a finish as possible is important, the ends can be glued down. The ends should be tied in a tight knot, then cut to about $\frac{1}{4}$in (6mm). Select the most appropriate ring or chain to lie the end along, lightly glue it and place the end carefully along it, holding it in place until secure. Repeat with the other end.

Glues

Selecting the best glue is important and obviously it is preferable to test the glues before using them. However, some glues deteriorate or discolour only after some time. Two glues which have remained satisfactory for at least two years are Elmers School Glue and the clear tubed adhesives such as Uhu. The white washable school glue, which dries colourless and with only a slight dulling of the thread colour, is very easy to work with. Squeeze out a small amount of glue onto a piece of paper and, using a cocktail stick, 'paint' the piece of tatting which is to be stuck. However, remember that this glue is water soluble and if the tatting is to be washed or thoroughly damped down for finishing then the ends will come away. The colourless adhesives in tubes stick well and dry with just a slight shine but they are difficult to work with on such things as pictures because of 'stringing' and the difficulty in controlling the flow of glue. A small amount can be put onto a piece of paper and used with a cocktail stick but it dries up very quickly.

Shaping and pressing tatting

After the ends have been finished the tatting will need some attention for it to lie flat and even. To shape the tatting, damp it well and carefully pull out all the picots evenly with a blunt needle, pull the rings so that they lie in the directions required, and shape the chains so that they curve evenly and neatly. Pressure from the hands may be sufficient to flatten the work but if it is not the piece can be pinned out and left to dry as shown in Illustration 11. The work can be ironed after shaping but this does tend to flatten the stitches and care must also be taken that the iron does not rub on the stitches and make them shiny. If the tatting needs to be stiffened then it can be sprayed with starch after shaping and just left to dry.

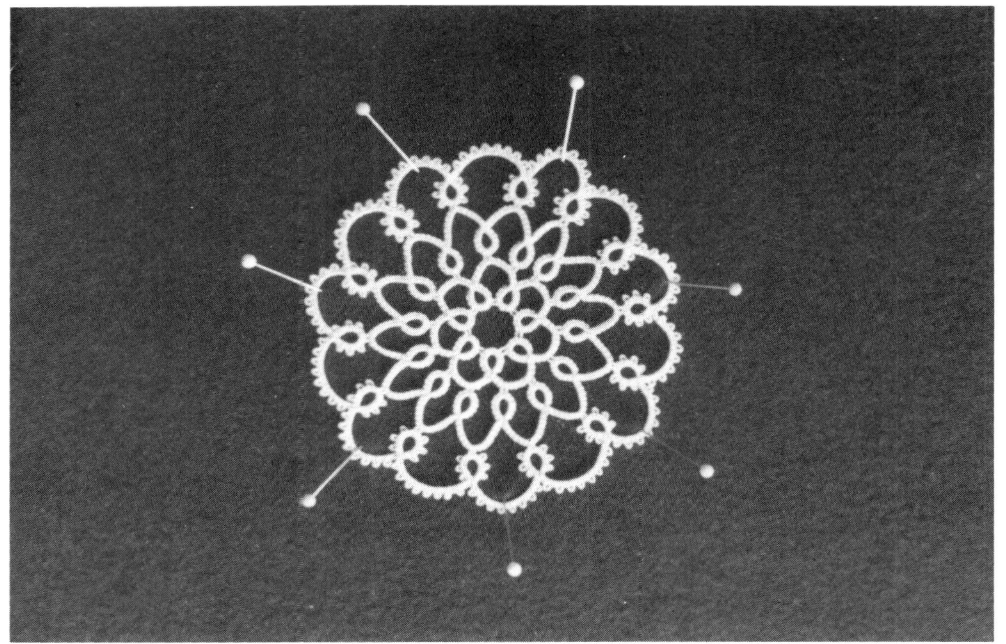

11 A piece of tatting which has been pinned out after damping and shaping

ABBREVIATIONS OF TATTING AND CROCHET TERMS

These abbreviations are used in the projects. Detailed explanations of the terms are given in the projects as their use occurs.

Tatting abbreviations

ds	double stitch
r	ring
ch	chain
cl	close
p	picot
sm p	small picot
l p	long picot
RW	reverse the work
JK	Josephine knot
sp	space
sep	separated
beg	beginning
tog	together
rep	repeat
rep from *	the portion of the pattern following the last preceding asterisk is to be worked, and then that portion is to be repeated as many times as stated.

Crochet abbreviations

dc	double crochet
ch	chain
yrh	yarn round the hook
ss	slip stitch

PATTERNS

Before moving onto the projects, patterns and what information they give need to be considered. Basically they state whether a ring or a chain is to be made and how many stitches are to be put in it; in addition they state where the picots are to be placed and when to join sections together. Generally it is assumed that the worker will know when only the shuttle thread is to be used and when an additional thread will be needed. The size of the picots is not usually detailed nor whether they are decorative or joining picots. For both the experienced and the inexperienced worker a clear picture or diagram is invaluable in showing the route the pattern takes, where it joins, and which picots are to be used for joining and which are decorative, so that their size may be decided before work commences. In the patterns in this book guidance is given about preparing the threads, and diagrams and photographs accompany the traditionally written instructions.

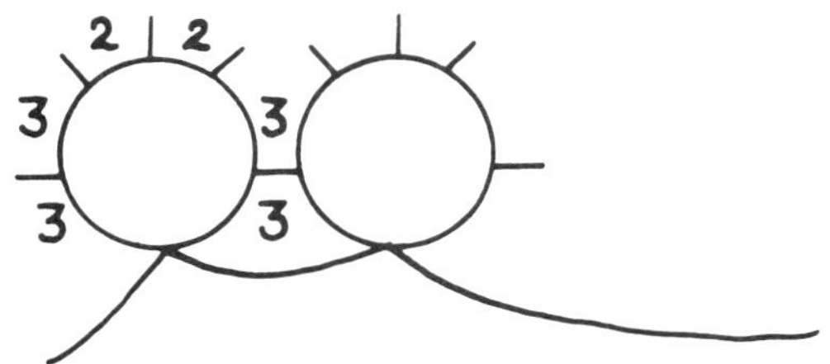

12 Diagram showing the construction details of a row of rings

How a pattern is written

The details of a ring of 3ds, p, 3ds, p, 2ds, p, 2ds, p, 3ds, p, 3ds, cl would be written in a pattern as 3ds, p, 3ds, 3p sep by 2ds, 3ds, p, 3ds, cl, and the next ring would read – leave ½in (12mm) thread, 3ds, join to last p of previous r, 3ds, 3p sep by 2ds, 3ds, p, 3ds, cl.

These construction details are shown in illustration 12. From this it can be seen that the pattern refers to a row of rings joined together by the fifth picot, whilst the second, third and fourth picots are decorative. Note that when a picot is formed, the double stitch involved in making the picot counts as one of the group of double stitches following the picot, e.g. 4ds, p, 4ds means a total of 8ds. Similarly, if picots are separated by 1ds, then that double stitch is the one produced in making the picot.

2 Basic Course

GIFT CARD

All the tatting on the card is made out of rings, with picots. Only shuttle thread is required. If one colour only is to be used then fill the shuttle before beginning work, but if different colours are to be used wind only a small amount onto the shuttle for each piece. For a special parcel use a piece of gold or silver card and make the tatted decorations with threads which pick out the colours of the wrapping paper.

Materials

No. 10 crochet thread
Piece of card, 3in × 5in (7.5cm × 12.5cm)
Two spacers, ½in and ¼in (12mm and 6mm) wide
Glue

Large flower

(make two)
Ring: (use the ½in (12mm) spacer when making the picots) 1ds, 10p sep by 1ds, 1ds, cl.
To finish: cut the working thread, leaving 3in (7.5cm) for the stem. Cut the thread left at the beginning to ¼in (6mm) and glue it neatly to one side.
Damp and flatten the tatting and leave to dry.

Small flower

(make three)
Ring: (use the ¼in (6mm) spacer when making the picots) 1ds, 6p sep by 1ds, 1ds, cl.
To finish: as large flower.

Clover leaf

(make three)
1st ring: leave 2in (5cm) thread at the start. 5ds, p, 5ds, cl.
2nd ring: close to the 1st r, 7ds, p, 7ds, cl.
3rd ring: close to the 2nd r, 5ds, p, 5ds, cl.

13 A gift card with flowers and leaves made of tatted rings with picots

To finish: cut the thread leaving 4in (10cm) for the stem. Tie the thread left at the start of the 1st r and the stem thread into a neat knot to keep the 1st and 3rd rings close together. Complete as large flower.

To complete the card

Prepare the card as detailed in the next section ('Preparing greetings cards'), so that it is folded in half to measure 3in × $2\frac{1}{2}$in (7.5cm × 6.25cm). Arrange the tatting as shown in Illustration 13, or as desired. Glue the backs of the pieces of tatting and carefully stick them onto the card. Trim the stems. Make a bow out of a piece of thread and glue it across the stems.

PREPARING GREETINGS CARDS

Attractive, individual greetings cards can be made effectively by sticking tatted flowers, or other motifs, onto blank cards which are available from stationers and art shops. These cards come in various sizes and colours and also with oval and other shaped cut-outs. However occasions arise when the size and colour of card needed is not available and to make the card oneself is the answer.

White and coloured card is available in different weights and usually comes in sheets of 20in by 30in (50cm by 75cm). Having decided on the approximate size of the finished greetings card you must select card of an appropriate weight, since large cards require a heavier weight of card than small ones if they are to stand satisfactorily. If the card will need an envelope it is best to start with the envelope and make the card to fit it, since suitable envelopes are not readily available in a good range of sizes.

To do justice to the time spent on the tatting, the card must be cut cleanly and straight, with all the corners at right angles. The best way of achieving this is to use a set-square; measure each side with a rule and mark the line to be cut with a sharp pencil. Remember that the cut piece of card must be twice the width and the same height as the finished card size (if it is to stand upright), or twice the height and the same width as the finished size (if it is to stand with the opening downwards). Straighter edges will

14 A selection of handmade cards

15 Equipment for preparing cards

be achieved if the sides are cut with a sharp craft knife. For safety's sake a metal rule, as shown in Illustration 15, should be used to guide the knife, and the card should be placed on a board or thick magazine before being cut. To ensure a crisp fold, measure and mark where the fold is to be then score the mark with a blunt knife.

HANDKERCHIEF EDGING

This edging is worked in a finer thread, a No. 20 crochet cotton which is available in a good selection of colours. The edging is composed of alternate large and small rings, all the rings joining one to another. Sufficient thread must be left between the rings for the work to form a straight edge. The rings should be pulled up firmly so that they look neat and have a good regular shape, and also so that they do not come open when the edging is pulled straight. Before starting the edging practise joining a few rings. The rings are joined by picots. The first ring with two picots coming off it is completed and then during its construction the second ring is joined to the last picot of the first ring (see Illustration 17).

To practise joining rings

1st ring: 4ds, p, 8ds, p, 4ds, cl.
2nd ring: leave ½in (12mm) thread, 4ds, join to last p of previous r. This is done by holding the 1st r at the side of the incomplete 2nd r, so that the last p of the 1st r is close to the thread on the fingers making the 2nd r – the ring thread. With the hook of the shuttle or a separate hook, go down through the picot and pick up the ring thread from right to left, pull a loop through the p and pass the shuttle through it. Now hold the shuttle thread taut and still, and gently regain tension on the left hand, manoeuvring the joining stitch so that it lies neatly. Check that the join has been made correctly and that the ring can be made larger or smaller.
Complete the second r by working 8ds, p, 4ds, cl. Repeat the instructions for the 2nd ring until the joins can be made with ease.

Joining a new thread

The shuttle will not hold sufficient thread to complete the edging. When more thread is needed simply cut off the old thread at the end of a ring, leaving an end of about 4in

(10cm) on the work. Refill the shuttle and with this new thread start the next ring and join it to the last ring made, in the usual way.

16 Handkerchief with an edging of large and small rings

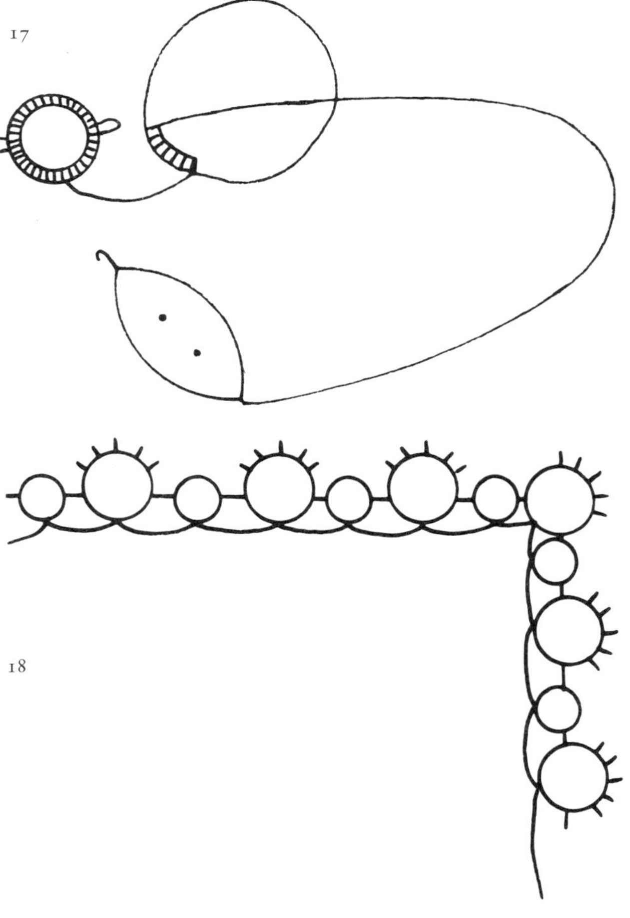

17 The positions of two rings about to be joined during the construction of the second ring

18 Diagram showing the construction of the handkerchief edging

Materials

No. 20 crochet thread in selected colour
One handkerchief

Making the edging

Fill the shuttle.

Small ring: 3ds, p, 6ds, p, 3ds, cl.

* *Large ring:* leave $\frac{1}{4}$in (6mm) thread, 3ds, join to last p of previous small r, 3ds, 5p sep by 2ds, 3ds, p, 3ds, cl.

Small ring: leave $\frac{1}{4}$in (6mm) thread, 3ds, join to last p of previous large r, 6ds, p, 3ds, cl.

Repeat from * until 4in (10cm) has been worked, then make a *corner* by making the next large and small rings as close together as possible. Rep from * along the full length of the next side and then make another corner. Complete the edging in this manner.

To finish

(See the section on 'Finishing ends'.) Where a new thread was started tie the two ends together in a firm knot close to the base of one of the rings. Sew all the ends neatly to one side.

Using a sewing thread the same colour as the handkerchief, carefully catch the tatting by the thread left between the rings to the edge of the handkerchief. Damp the work, pull into shape and press dry.

MOTIF BIRTHDAY CARD

Motifs of rings and chains

Motifs have many uses. They can be used as decorations on the corners of handkerchiefs or on clothing, on pockets and collars. Motifs can be joined together to make a larger piece of tatting for such things as

19 Birthday card of tatted flowers

cloths, bags and shawls. Further rounds can be added to a single motif to make a larger decoration or mat. In the birthday card, the motifs are made into flowers with the addition of a chain stem but the same patterns can be used as decorations simply by omitting this stem. The motifs combine rings and chains, and to make them two threads are required. The rings are made with the thread from the shuttle, and the chains are made from the second thread, from the ball. However the shuttle thread is also involved in the construction of the chains as was seen when the double stitch was learnt.

Reversing the work (RW)

When rings and chains are combined, the piece of tatting is reversed (or turned over) between each ring, or set of rings, and the following chain. It is then reversed back again before starting the next ring. This process can be easily learnt and practised whilst making the motifs for the card.

First a ring is made. Note the position of the ring and the threads on completion of the first ring before a chain is made, in Illustration 20.

The work is then reversed ready for making the chain stitches with thread from the ball. Note the position of the ring and the threads after the work has been reversed in Illustration 21.

When the chain is completed the work is reversed again before making the next ring, as in Illustration 22.

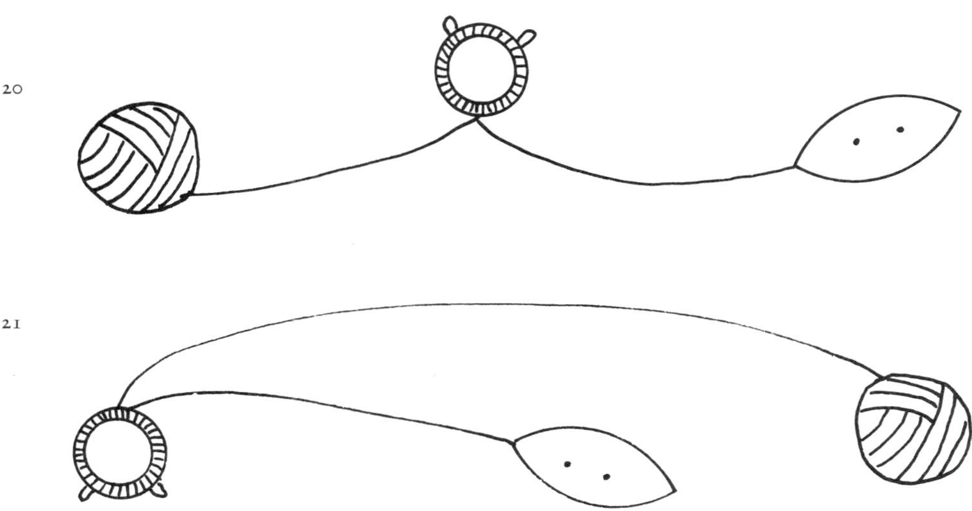

20

21

22

Materials

No. 20 crochet thread in selected colour(s)
12in (30cm) narrow ribbon
Piece of card, approximately 8in × 5½in (20cm × 14cm)
Piece of contrasting colour card, approximately 3¼in × 4¾in (8.5cm × 12cm)
To avoid unnecessary ends it is best to start with an unbroken thread between the ball and shuttle whenever possible.

Motif 1

(Illustration 23)

Measure 5ft (150cm) thread off the ball but do not cut off. Wind almost all of this measured amount onto the shuttle and prepare to start the 1st ring by winding the thread between the ball and the shuttle, round the hand. Work this ring in the usual way, ignoring the ball thread.

1st ring: 5ds, p, 3ds, p, 5ds, cl. RW so that the work is in the position shown in Illustration 21. Grasp the ring between the thumb and forefinger of the left hand, hold the thread from the ball over the fingers of the same hand (as detailed in the construction of the ds on a chain) and then, with the shuttle, make a chain by working ds on the ball thread.

* *Chain:* 10ds. RW so that the work is in the position shown in Illustration 22.

Ring: 5ds, join to the adjacent p of the previous r, 3ds, p, 5ds, cl. RW.

Rep from * 3 times.

5th chain: 10ds. RW.

6th ring: 5ds, join to the adjacent p of the previous r, 3ds, join to the free p of the 1st r, 5ds, cl. RW.

6th chain: 10ds, join to the 1st chain, where it was started at the base of the 1st ring. Continue without cutting the thread to make the stem chain.

Stem chain: make ds until the stem measures 4in (10cm). Cut the ends leaving 2in (5cm) thread, tie an overhand knot close to the last ds and trim the ends close to this knot.

Motif 2

(Illustration 24)

Prepare the threads as for the first motif.

1st ring: 3ds, 3p sep by 3ds, 3ds, cl. RW.

* *Chain:* 3ds, 3p sep by 3ds, 3ds. RW.

Ring: 3ds, join to last p of previous r, 3ds, 2p sep by 3ds, 3ds, cl. RW.

Rep from * until 4 rings and chains have been made.

5th ring: 3ds, join to last p of previous r, 3ds, p, 3ds, join to 1st p of 1st r, 3ds, cl. RW.

5th chain: as previous ch, join to 1st ch at base of 1st r. Continue into stem, and complete as motif 1.

Motif 3

(Illustration 25)

Prepare the threads as for the first motif.

1st ring: 6ds, sm p, 1ds, sm p, 6ds, cl. RW.

1st chain: 3ds, p, 4ds, p, 3ds. RW.

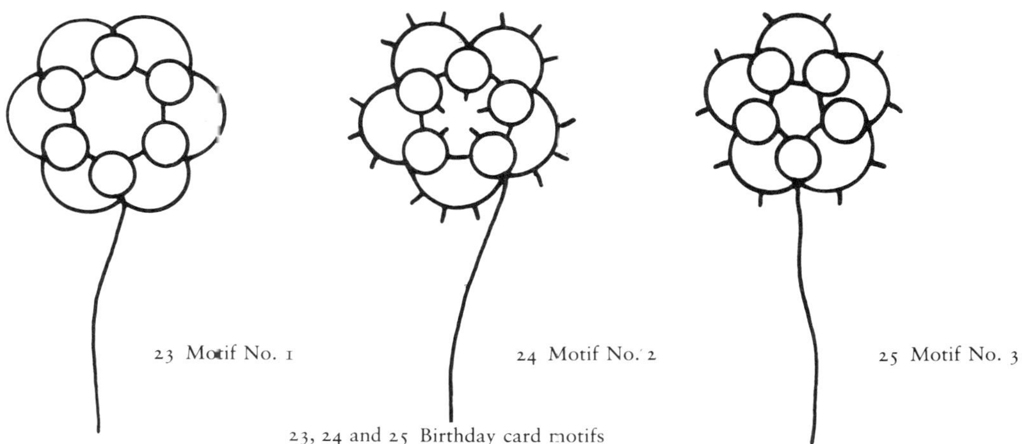

23 Motif No. 1

24 Motif No. 2

25 Motif No. 3

23, 24 and 25 Birthday card motifs

* *Next ring:* 6ds, join to last sm p of previous r, 1ds, sm p, 6ds, cl. RW.
Next chain: As 1st ch.
Rep from * twice.
Last ring: 6ds, join to last sm p of previous r, 1ds, join to 1st sm p of 1st r, 6ds, cl. RW.
Last chain: As 1st ch, join to 1st ch at base of 1st r. Continue into stem and complete as motif 1.

The three small flowers

These are rings with picots and a single thread forming the stem.
No. 1: ring: 1ds, 11p sep by 1ds, 1ds, cl. Cut ends leaving 4in (10cm) for the stem, cut the other end to $\frac{1}{4}$in (6mm) and glue it to the back.
No. 2: ring: 1ds, 7p sep by 1ds, 1ds, cl. Complete as No. 1.
No. 3: ring: 1ds, 7 l p sep by 1ds, 1ds, cl. Complete as No. 1.

To complete the card

Damp the flowers, shape and allow to dry. Prepare the card, as detailed in the section 'Preparing greetings cards', so that the card is folded in half to 4in × $5\frac{1}{2}$in (10cm × 14cm). Write the greeting on the top right-hand side of the piece of contrasting card and glue it centrally to the prepared card. Plan the arrangement of the flowers and carefully glue them in place, gathering all the stems together. Trim the stems if necessary. Tie the ribbon in a bow and glue over the stems.

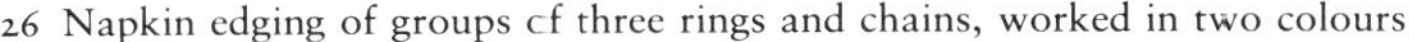

26 Napkin edging of groups of three rings and chains, worked in two colours

NAPKIN EDGING IN TWO COLOURS

It has been seen that alternating rings and chains can form motifs but they can also be made into straight edgings providing the picots are placed appropriately in the joining rings. Motifs and edgings can also be made where groups of rings are followed by a chain.

So the sequence of a pattern may well be (ring, chain), (ring, chain), . . . (illustration 27), but it could also be (ring, chain, ring), (ring, chain, ring), . . . (illustration 28), and in the case of the napkin edging (ring 1, ring 2, ring 3, chain), (ring 1, ring 2, ring 3, chain), . . . (illustration 29). In the last two examples the work would only be reversed immediately before and after the chains, i.e. not between rings.

Working with two colours

Since rings are made completely with the shuttle thread and the stitches of the chains are made with the ball thread, the colour of the rings and chains need not be the same. Whatever colour is wound onto the shuttle will be the colour of the rings and the colour of the ball thread will be the colour of the chains.

Materials

No. 20 crochet thread in two colours
Napkin

Measurements

Depth of edging – ¾in (18mm)

Making the edging

Fill the shuttle with one colour and have ready a ball of the second colour. In the first ring weave in the end of the shuttle thread after making the first stitch. On the first chain make the first stitch close to the base of the third ring, then weave in the end of the ball thread along the chain.

1st ring: 9ds, p, 6ds, p, 3ds, cl.
* *2nd ring:* close to 1st r, 3ds, join to last p of 1st r, 3ds, 5p sep by 2ds, 3ds, p, 3ds, cl.
3rd ring: close to 2nd r, 3ds, join to last p of 2nd r, 6ds, p, 9ds, cl. RW.
Chain: 3ds, 5p sep by 3ds, 3ds. RW.
1st ring: 9ds, join to last p of previous 3rd r, 6ds, p, 3ds, cl.

Rep from * until the shuttle thread is almost finished. Leaving about 4in (10cm) attached to the work, cut the shuttle thread off at the end of a 1st or 2nd ring or after the chain. Refill the shuttle and make the next ring, weaving in the end and joining as before. Tightly knot the remaining piece of the old shuttle thread to the new shuttle thread at the base of the ring just made and weave the end into the next chain.

Continue with the edging until it is almost long enough to go round the napkin, sew it into position by the centre picots of the chains, then complete the final section joining the last ring to the first ring made and the last chain to the first chain. Finish attaching the edging to the napkin and sew down the two final ends. Damp and shape the work and press flat.

SET OF COASTERS

These mats start with a central motif to which further rounds are added. At the end of the centre and also at the end of each round, the threads must be cut and new threads prepared for the next stage. To avoid wasting thread, in the early stages particularly, note how many rings are to be made and estimate the length of shuttle thread which will be required. The rings with six picots will take more thread than those without picots. The large mat is made by adding two further rounds to the small mat pattern.

Materials

No. 20 crochet thread in selected colour

Measurements

Small mat – $3\frac{3}{4}$in (9.5cm)
Large mat – $6\frac{1}{4}$in (15.6cm)

30 Set of coasters

Small mat

Centre motif

Wind enough thread onto the shuttle to make seven rings and a little more for the chains, but do not cut off from the ball.
1st ring: 5ds, p, 3ds, p, 5ds, cl. RW.
1st chain: 3ds, p, 5ds, p, 3ds. RW.
* *Next ring:* 5ds, join to last p of previous r, 3ds, p, 5ds, cl. RW.
Next chain: as 1st ch.

Rep from * until 6 rings and chains have been made.
7th ring: 5ds, join to last p of previous r, 3ds, join to free p of 1st r, 5ds, cl. RW.
7th chain: As 1st ch, join to 1st ch at base of 1st r. Tie ends and cut.

31 An enlarged view of the coasters to show the construction

1st round
Wind enough thread onto the shuttle to make 14 rings and chains, but do not cut off from the ball.
1st ring: 7ds, join to a p of any ch on the centre, 7ds, cl. RW.
1st chain: 7ds, p, 7ds. RW.
* *Next ring:* 7ds, join to next p on the centre, 7ds, cl. RW.
Next chain: as 1st ch.

Rep from * until all the picots of the centre have been used, end by joining the last ch to the 1st ch at the base of the 1st r. Tie ends and cut.

2nd round
Wind enough thread onto the shuttle to make 14 rings with picots and 14 chains, but do not cut off from the ball.
1st ring: 2ds, 3p sep by 2ds, 2ds, join to the p of any ch on the previous round, 2ds, 3p sep by 2ds, 2ds, cl. RW.
1st chain: 2ds, 8p sep by 2ds, 2ds. RW.
* *Next ring:* 2ds, 3p sep by 2ds, 2ds, join to the p of the next ch on the previous round, 2ds, 3p sep by 2ds, 2ds, cl. RW.
Next chain: as 1st ch.

Rep from * until all the picots of the previous round have been used, end by joining the last ch to the 1st ch at the base of the 1st r. Tie ends and cut.

To finish
Sew all ends neatly to one side. Damp the work and pull into shape, pinning out the chains if necessary so that the mat is circular. When dry stiffen with spray starch and leave to dry.

Large mat
Work as instructed for small mat and then continue with the 3rd and 4th rounds.

3rd round
This round has 28 rings and chains. Fill the shuttle but do not cut off from the ball.
1st ring: 7ds, join to the 3rd p from the left, of any ch on the 2nd round, 7ds, cl. RW.

1st chain: 7ds, p, 7ds. RW.
* *Next ring:* 7ds, join to the 6th p of the same ch on the 2nd round, 7ds, cl. RW.
Next chain: as 1st ch.
Next ring: 7ds, join to the 3rd p of the next ch, 7ds, cl. RW.
Next chain: as 1st ch.

Rep from * until 2 rings have been joined to each chain on the 2nd round, join the last ch to the 1st ch at the base of the 1st r. Tie ends and cut.

4th round
This round has 28 rings with picots and 28 chains. Fill the shuttle but do not cut off from the ball.

Work as instructed for the 2nd round of the small mat.

Finish as instructed for the small mat.

32 Motifs attached to velvet ribbon and used for bookmarks

BOOKMARK MOTIFS

These motifs introduce some new construction techniques. They are worked in a finer thread than the previous pieces and each is attached to a length of velvet ribbon.

Materials
No. 40 crochet thread in selected colour
For each bookmark, a piece of velvet ribbon $\frac{3}{8}$in × 8in (1cm × 21cm)
Two shuttles for the second motif

Measurements
Both motifs – $1\frac{1}{2}$in (3.7cm) diameter

Double edged motif
(Illustration 33)
The rings in the centre of this motif are all joined into one long picot which comes off the first ring made. This picot must be long enough for five rings to join into it, but not so long that there is a lot of spare thread. Judging the correct length of picot comes with practise. The chains of the 1st round are made alternately with the rings, then the chains of the 2nd round are made without breaking the threads and they join into the space between the chains of the 1st round.

Centre motif
Wind a small amount of thread onto the shuttle, but do not cut off from the ball.
1st ring: 3ds, p, 6ds, l p, 6ds, p, 3ds, cl. RW.
1st chain: 2ds, 5p sep by 2ds, 2ds. RW.
* *Next ring:* 3ds, p, 6ds, join to the l p of the 1st r, 6ds, p, 3ds, cl. RW.
Next chain: as 1st ch.

Rep from * 4 times, join the last ch to the 1st ch at the base of the 1st r. Continue with an unbroken thread into the 2nd round.

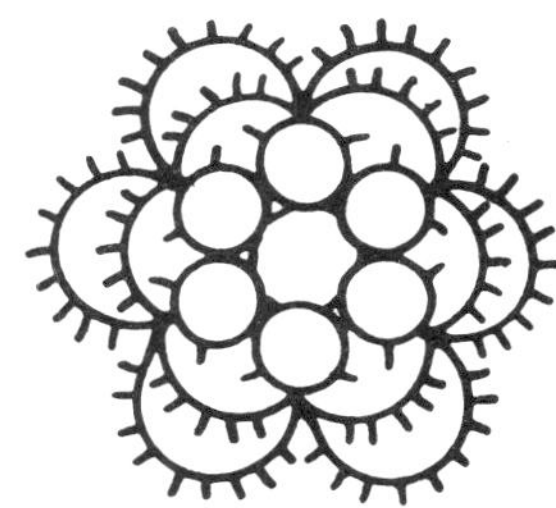

33 Double edged motif

2nd round
* *Chain:* 2ds, 9p sep by 2ds, 2ds, join to the sp between the chains of the centre motif. Rep from * 5 times. Tie ends and cut short.

To complete the bookmark
Glue the ends neatly to one side. Starch and shape the motif and leave to dry. Take the length of velvet ribbon and spread a little clear glue over the back of each end to prevent it fraying. Glue one set of chains to one end of the velvet, making sure the motif lies evenly.

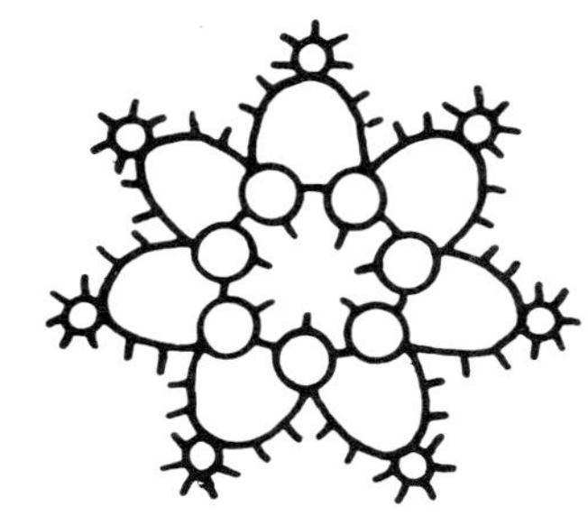
34 Motif worked with two shuttles

35 Two shuttles wound with an unbroken thread and numbered for identification during work

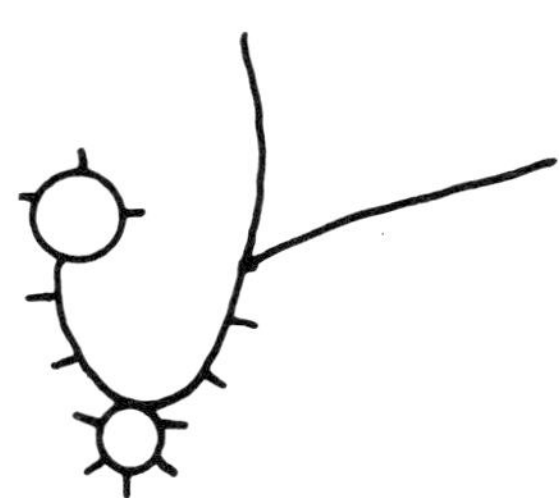
36 Diagram showing the beginning of the two shuttle motif, after the 1st centre ring and 1st chain have been worked

Two shuttle motif

(Illustration 34)
Working with two shuttles, instead of one shuttle and a ball thread, generally allows greater flexibility and the neater working of some patterns. Additionally it makes it possible to have rings coming off the picot side of a chain whilst maintaining the smooth line of that chain. Two shuttles must be wound and it is preferable to have an unbroken thread between them. It may be helpful at first to mark the shuttles '1' and '2' with a piece of sticky tape.

Measure $3\frac{1}{2}$ yards (3m) of thread from the ball and cut. Find the centre of this length and mark it. Attach one end of the thread to shuttle 1 and wind half the thread onto it. Attach the other end of the thread to shuttle 2 and wind the other half of the thread onto that, as shown in Illustration 35.
Use shuttle 1 as usual and shuttle 2 as if it were the ball thread.

1st centre ring: 3ds, p, 2ds, p, 2ds, p, 3ds, cl. RW. Continue to use shuttle 1 as normal.
1st chain: 2ds, p, 2ds, p, 2ds, *do not reverse*, drop shuttle 1 and using shuttle 2 make a *small ring* of 2ds, 5p sep by 1ds, 2ds, cl, *do not reverse*, drop shuttle 2 and using shuttle 1 complete the *chain*, 2ds, p, 2ds, p, 2ds. RW. (See Illustration 36.)
* *Next centre ring:* 3ds, join to the last p of the previous centre r, 2ds, p, 2ds, p, 3ds, cl. RW.
Next chain: as 1st ch.
Rep from * 4 times.
Last centre ring (7th): 3ds, join to last p of the previous centre r, 2ds, p, 2ds, join to the 1st p of the 1st centre r, 3ds, cl. RW.
Last chain: as 1st ch, join to the 1st ch at the base of the 1st centre r. Tie ends and cut short.

To complete the bookmark
Prepare the motif and the velvet as for the

double edged motif but glue one small ring and a little of the chain to the centre of one end of the velvet.

BOOKMARK BRAID WITH JOSEPHINE KNOTS

Josephine knots are small rings made by repeating only one half of the double stitch. Either the first half or the second half of the stitch can be used but the rings may pull up more easily when the second half is used. Josephine knots have a flatter, smoother appearance than rings of the same size made with the whole double stitch. On the bookmark braid the Josephine knots are replacing picots as decoration on the chains and so, in order to produce a smooth line on the chains, two shuttles are used in the construction of the braid.

Materials

No. 20 crochet thread in selected colour
Two shuttles

Measurements

9in × $1\frac{1}{2}$in (22.5cm × 3.7cm)

Completely fill one shuttle – to avoid a join at the beginning of the work do not cut the thread but unwind a similar amount from the ball and cut, then starting from the cut end fill the second shuttle with the unwound thread.

First side

Use one shuttle as usual and the second in place of the ball thread. The 1st large ring at the start of the pattern is marked 1 on the diagram at Illustration 38.
1st large ring: 3ds, 9p sep by 3ds, 3ds, cl. RW.
1st chain: 4ds, drop the 1st shuttle, pick up the 2nd and make a Josephine knot of 10 half stitches (JK 10), then with the 1st shuttle complete the chain with 4ds. RW.
1st small ring: 3ds, p, 3ds, join to the 8th p of the 1st large ring, 3ds, 3p sep by 3ds, 3ds, cl. RW.
* *Next chain:* as 1st ch.
Next large ring: 3ds, p, 3ds, join to the 4th p of the previous small ring, 3ds, 7p sep by 3ds,

37 Bookmark braid with Josephine knots

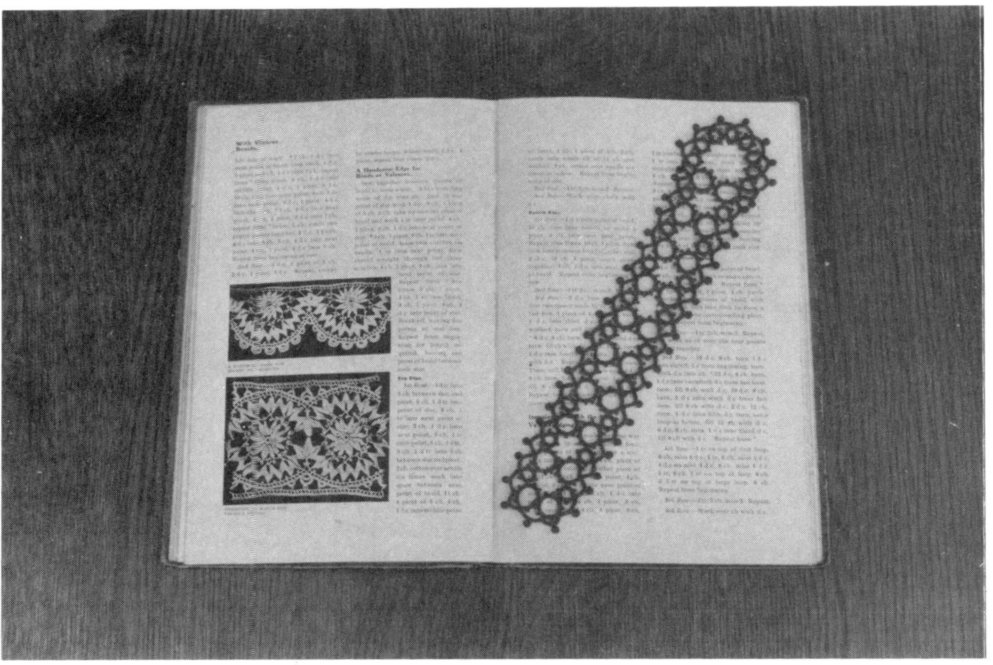

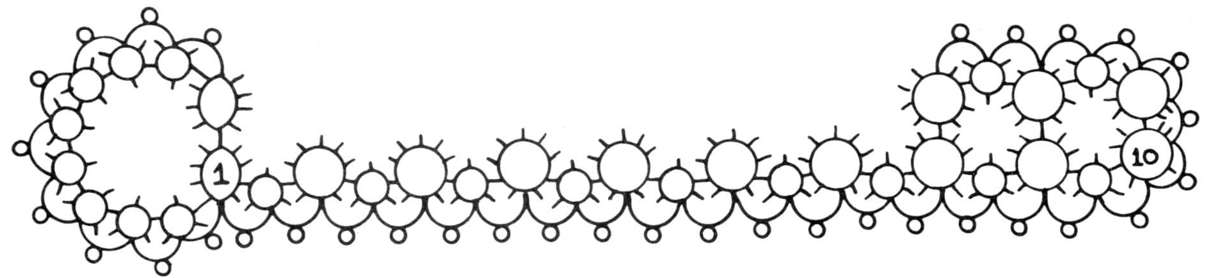

38 Diagram showing construction details of the Bookmark braid

3ds, cl. RW.
Next chain: as 1st ch.
Next small ring: as 1st small r.

Rep from * 7 times and then make one further ch and large r. RW.

Bottom end

Chain: 4ds, JK 10, 4ds, join to the 8th p of the previous large r (marked 10 on Illustration 38).
Chain: 4ds, JK 10, 4ds. RW.
Large ring: 3ds, 2p sep by 3ds, 3ds, join to the 5th p of the previous large ring, 3ds, 6p sep by 3ds, 3ds, cl. RW.
Chain: 4ds, JK 10, 4ds, join to the 8th p of the previous large ring.
Chain: 4ds, JK 10, 4ds. RW.

Second side

Small ring: 3ds, p, 3ds, join to the 6th p of the previous large ring, 3ds, 3p sep by 3ds, 3ds, cl. RW.
* *Chain:* 4ds, JK 10, 4ds. RW.
Large ring: 3ds, p, 3ds, join to the 4th p of the previous small r, 3ds, 2p sep by 3ds, 3ds, join to the 5th p of the large r opposite on the 1st side, 3ds, 4p sep by 3ds, 3ds, cl. RW.
Chain: 4ds, JK 10, 4ds. RW.
Small ring: 3ds, p, 3ds, join to the 8th p of the previous large r, 3ds, 3p sep by 3ds, 3ds, cl. RW.

Rep from * 7 times and then make one further ch and large r – which joins to the last r on the 1st side.

Top

1st chain: 4ds, JK 10, 4ds. RW.
Small ring: 3ds, p, 3ds, join to the 9th p of the previous large r, 3ds, 3p sep by 3ds, 3ds, cl. RW.
Chain: as 1st ch.
* *Small ring:* 3ds, p, 3ds, join to the 4th p of the previous small r, 3ds, 3p sep by 3ds, 3ds, cl. RW.
Chain: as 1st ch.

Rep from * 5 times.

Small ring: 3ds, p, 3ds, join to the 4th p of the previous small r, 3ds, p, 3ds, join to the 1st p of the 1st large r made on the 1st side, 3ds, p, 3ds, cl. RW.
Chain: as 1st ch, join to the 1st ch made, at the base of the 1st r on the 1st side. Tie ends and cut.

To finish

Glue or sew all ends neatly to one side. Starch and shape the braid, paying particular attention to the chains.

CHRISTMAS DECORATIONS OR SHADE PULLS

A covered curtain ring gives these medallions weight and helps them keep their shape when in use. A twisted cord is attached to the medallions for use as shade pulls. The central, tatted motif is joined to the curtain ring at the same time as the ring is being covered with double crochet or with buttonhole stitch. Any motif which will fit inside the selected size of ring is suitable, but it should have picots on the outer edge by which to attach it to the ring. The tatted edging is worked directly onto the covered ring. The medallions look well when the ring is covered in a contrasting colour.

Materials

No. 20 crochet thread in selected colour(s)
No. 1.00mm crochet hook or sewing needle
Curtain ring, 1¼in (3cm) internal diameter, for each medallion

Measurements

Medallion 1 – 2in (5cm) diameter
Medallion 2 – 2¼in (5.5cm) diameter
Cord – 12in (30cm) long

Medallion 1

(Illustration 39)

Centre motif

1st ring: 8ds, p long enough for the next 4 rings to join into, 8ds, cl. RW.
1st chain: 4ds, p, 4ds, p, 4ds. RW.
* *Next ring:* 8ds, join to l p of 1st r, 8ds, cl. RW.
Next chain: as 1st ch.

Rep from * 3 times, join the last ch to the 1st ch at the base of the 1st r. Tie ends and cut.

Joining the motif to the curtain ring with double crochet

The use of a No. 1.00mm crochet hook will produce a neat double crochet stitch which will be sufficiently loose for the tatting to be joined easily into it. Using the ball thread, put a loop on the hook. Holding the curtain ring in the left hand, put the working thread over the top of the ring and have the hook at the front of the ring. Put the hook into the ring, catch the thread and pull a loop through (two loops on the hook), yrh and pull through both loops, 1st stitch made. The 'bars' at the top of the dc stitches lie around the outside of the ring. Continue covering the ring with tight and neat dc for about ¼in (6mm), * then take the tatted motif and work the next dc through a p on the ch and over the ring, thus beginning to join the motif to the ring. Work a sufficient number of dc over the ring so that the ring is well covered and the next p can be joined without distorting the shape of the motif. Complete the joining of the motif in this manner, then finish covering the ring and join into the 1st dc with a ss. Fasten off and cut the thread.

39 Medallion 1 shown with a twisted cord for use as a shade pull

Joining the motif to the curtain ring with buttonhole stitch

Using a needle and a long length of doubled thread, cover the ring neatly with buttonhole stitch for about ¼in (6mm). The 'bars' of the stitches will lie around the outside of the ring. Now continue working from the crochet instructions from *, replacing

40 Medallion 2 with a loop hanger for use as a Christmas decoration

any references to 'dc' with 'buttonhole stitch(es)'.

Edging

Wind a small amount of thread onto the shuttle and do not cut off from the ball. Join into a dc or buttonhole stitch on the covered ring in the same way as joining into a picot.
*1st round: * chain:* 7ds, allowing the ch to curve as desired, join into a dc or buttonhole stitch on the ring. Rep from * all round the ring taking care with the spacing at the end.
*2nd round: * chain:* 4ds, 3p sep by 1ds, 4ds, join to the sp between the ch of the 1st round. Rep from * all round.

To complete

Tie ends and cut leaving long ends for hanging if using for a decoration. Make a twisted cord if using for a shade pull. Glue or sew all ends to one side.

Twisted cord

Cut a length of thread $4\frac{1}{2}$yd (4m) long and fold it in half and then half again. Tie the loose ends together with an overhand knot and anchor this knot firmly so that the thread may be held taut. Hold the other end of the thread and insert a pencil into the loop at that end. Keeping the thread taut, twist the pencil until the whole length of thread is tightly twisted. Still keeping the thread taut, grasp the centre, bring the two ends together and then release them, allowing the two halves to twist together to form the cord. Cut the loose end of the cord to the length required, knot it and sew to the medallion.

Medallion 2

(Illustration 40)

Centre motif

In this motif a ring with six long picots and five small picots is made first and then, without breaking the threads, chains are worked around that ring joining into the small picots. Wind a small amount of thread onto the shuttle but do not cut off from the ball.
Ring: * 1ds, l p, 1ds, sm p. Rep from * 4 times, 1ds, l p, 1ds, cl. RW.
Chain: sm p, * 2ds, 7p sep by 2ds, 2ds, join to next sm p on the r. Rep from * 5 times, join the last ch to the sm p made at the beginning of the round of chains. Tie ends and cut.

Join the motif to the curtain ring by the 4th p on each ch whilst covering the ring with double crochet or buttonhole stitch, as detailed in medallion 1.

Edging

Although the edging is constructed entirely of chains each alternate chain is joined to make it look like a ring. Using ball and shuttle thread join to the ring.
* *Chain:* 4ds, 3p sep by 1ds, 4ds, then, allowing the ch to arch, join to a stitch on the ring.

41 Mat made of 7 clover ring motifs. (*opposite*)

Chain: 4ds, 5p sep by 1ds, 4ds, join to same stitch as last join to form a mock ring.

Rep from * all round the ring, taking care with the spacing at the end. Complete as for medallion 1.

CLOVER RING MOTIF MAT

This mat is made out of small, six-sided motifs which are joined together as they are being worked. The shape of a finished motif mat will depend on the shape of the motifs, the number of motifs used and the way they are joined together. When planning motif mats it is interesting to find a motif which will form a pleasing secondary design when it is joined to other motifs. The mat shown in Illustration 41 is made out of seven motifs. The shape and motif positions of a larger mat using fourteen motifs is shown in Illustration 43.

Materials
No. 20 crochet thread in selected colour

Measurements
Each motif – 2in (5cm) diameter

Small mat
For each motif measure 3yd and 6in (3m) thread off the ball but do not cut off. Wind this measured amount of thread onto the shuttle.

1st motif
1st clover leaf:
Small ring: 6ds, p, 4ds, p, 2ds, cl.
Large ring: 2ds, join to last p of previous r, 8ds, p, 8ds, p, 2ds, cl.

42 Diagram of a single clover ring motif

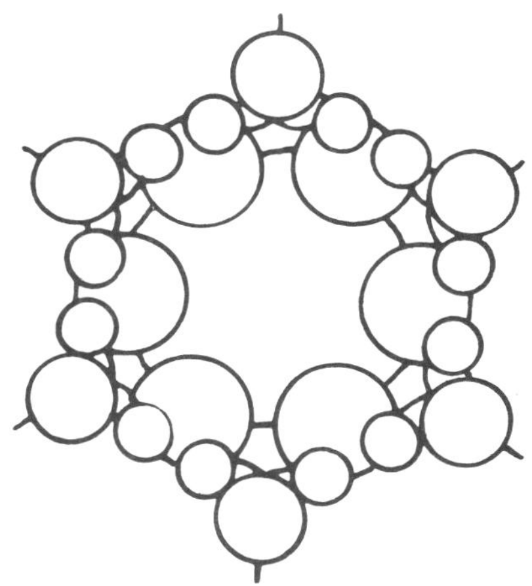

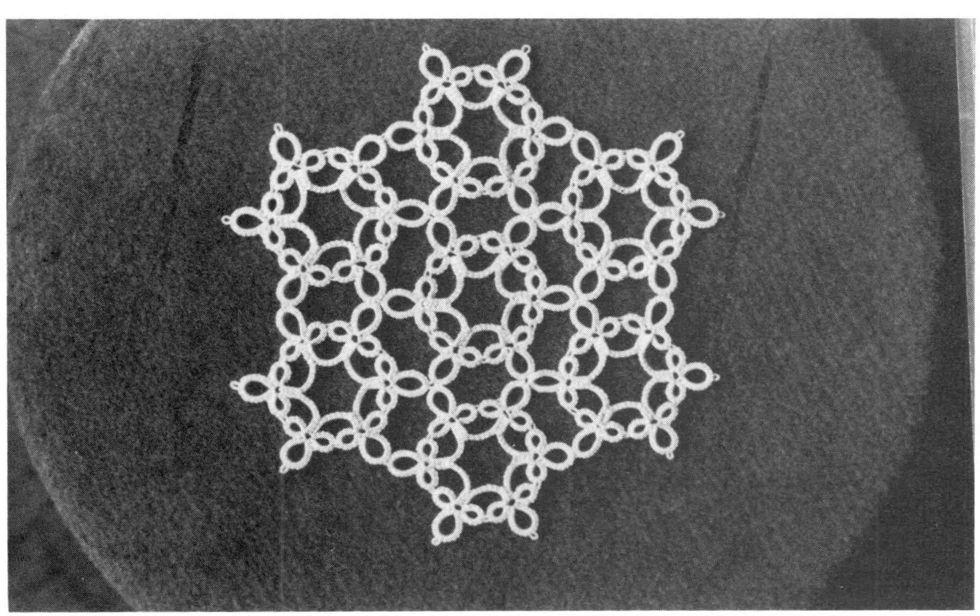

Small ring: 2ds, join to last p of previous r, 4ds, p, 6ds, cl. RW.
Chain: 3ds, sm p, 6ds, sm p, 3ds. RW.
* *Next clover leaf:*
Small ring: 6ds, join to last p of previous r, 4ds, p, 2ds, cl.
Large ring: 2ds, join to last p of previous r, 8ds, p, 8ds, p, 2ds, cl.
Small ring: 2ds, join to last p of previous r, 4ds, p, 6ds, cl. RW.
Chain: 3ds, join to last p of previous ch, 6ds, sm p, 3ds. RW.

Rep from * until 5 complete clover leaves have been made and the first two rings of the 6th, then complete the motif as follows. Because the motif has a circle of rings on the outside, the first and last rings can be difficult to join without twisting the last joining picot. One way to avoid the twist is to fold the first part of the motif back behind the ring being worked and then twist the joining picot downwards before joining into it.

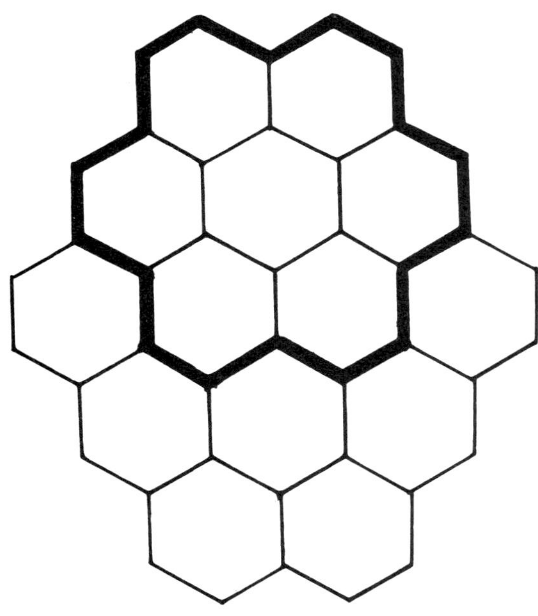

43 Diagram showing the position of the motifs for joining

Last small ring: 2ds, join to last p of previous r, 4ds, join to 1st p of 1st r made, 6ds, cl. RW.
Last chain: 3ds, join to p of previous ch, 6ds, join to free p of 1st ch, 3ds, join to the base of the 1st clover leaf. Tie ends and cut.

2nd motif

1st clover leaf:
Small ring: 6ds, p, 4ds, p, 2ds, cl.
Large ring: 2ds, join to last p of previous r, 8ds, join to p on a large r on 1st motif, 8ds, p, 2ds, cl.
Small ring: 2ds, join to last p of previous r, 4ds, p, 6ds, cl. RW.
Chain: 3ds, p, 6ds, p, 3ds. RW.
Next clover leaf:
Small ring: 6ds, join to last p of previous r, 4ds, p, 2ds, cl.
Large ring: 2ds, join to last p of previous r, 8ds, join to p of next large r on 1st motif, 8ds, p, 2ds, cl.

Complete as 1st motif.

Make five more motifs, joining in this manner and placing them as shown in Illustration 43, noting that where three motifs meet three large rings will be joined.

To finish

Sew down all ends securely, damp the work, shape the chains evenly and pull out the picots on the outside rings. Leave to dry then spray with starch to stiffen.

3 Using Beads and Sequins

INTRODUCTION TO BEADS

Beaded tatting

Beads seem to have a fascination all their own. They have been used for centuries; generation after generation has used them for personal adornment and has incorporated them into almost any handicraft you can think of to decorate an amazing variety of items. Tatting is no exception. Queen Marie of Romania was using beads and precious stones in her tatting in the early part of this century and produced some interesting and elaborate pieces, particularly for the church. In *The Priscilla Tatting Book*, published in 1915, beads are prominent, being used in some beautiful pieces of work ranging from jewellery and hair decorations to bags and braids. Rhoda L. Auld's book, *Tatting*, which was published in 1974, has some interesting ideas for using beads and an excellent chapter on the different techniques of tatting with beads.

Beads can be incorporated in tatting in many ways. They can be used, like picots, as a decoration on both rings and chains. They can be put into rings and between rings; can be put onto picots or added with a needle and thread after the tatting has been completed. In this book the four following projects each describe and use a different method of putting beads into tatting. Beads are included in several of the other patterns – in most of the jewellery, the round picture frame, the Misty Morn picture and the lavender bag – all using the techniques detailed in the earlier projects. Sequins can also be used in tatting to add colour and interest. Some general comments about working with sequins are given in the pattern for mobile medallions which are worked around sequins.

Selecting beads

Beads are available in a wonderful assortment of colours, sizes and shapes and are made of many different materials including glass, wood, clay and plastic. Deciding which type of bead to use is important so consider why they are being used. Are they to be the main feature of the piece of work? Perhaps they are to be used as an interesting contrast to the thread colour, or maybe only as a highlight. They may be used to add weight. Size is important, as a large bead on a fine piece of tatting may pull the piece out of shape or just look too heavy, equally very small beads can look insignificant on tatting worked in a thick thread. Sizes of beads in one packet, particularly the small glass ones, can vary enormously and this must be taken into account – do the beads need to be uniform in size or would a variation in shape be attractive and acceptable? Different shapes of beads lie in different ways and particular care should be taken that those worked in clusters lie well together.

Consideration must also be given to the fact that the colour of some beads is adversely affected by water, starch and perspiration

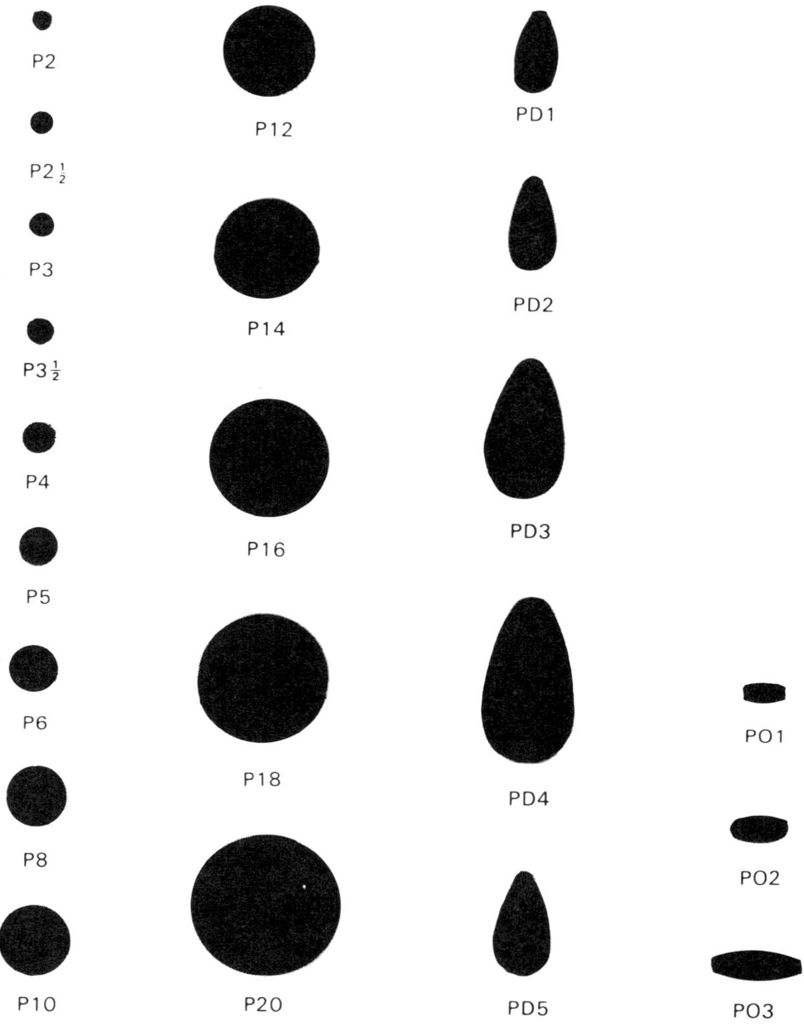

Pearls Articles P2-P12 and Pearl oats articles PO1-PO3 all have through centre hole.
Pearl Drops articles PD1-PD4 all have their hole top to bottom article PD5 has hole across top.
Pearls – the number following prefix P is size of article in millimetres.

44 The selection of pearls and pearl drops taken from Creative Beadcraft Ltd's catalogue, with permission.
Colour range
1. White
2. Gold metallic
3. Silver metallic
4. Cream
5. Pink
6. Lilac
7. Turquoise
8. Blue
(Most, but not all, beads available in each colour.)

(even perspiration from the hands whilst working), and beads which may be subjected to any of these things should be tested before beginning work. If the item is to be washed then the composition of the bead may be adversely affected.

The range of sizes, shapes and colours of just one type of bead are shown in the page of pearls and pearl drops taken from Creative Beadcraft Ltd's catalogue (Illustration 44). The majority of the bead projects in this book use beads from this range. They are uniform in size, are available in strings of 100 and to date have been unaffected by water, starch and handling. There may, however, be slight variations in colour in different batches and sufficient beads of the same colour should be purchased before beginning projects. If different beads are to be used when working the projects their size can be checked by holding the alternative bead over those illustrated which are actual size.

Tatting with beads

After selecting the beads and the thread to be used the next task is to plan where the beads are to appear. This is necessary because beads which are to decorate a chain must be threaded onto the ball thread before work commences. They are incorporated into the work when required by being pushed along the ball thread close to the last stitch made, and held in place by the next stitch which should be close to the bead. Beads which are to be on a ring must be put onto the shuttle thread and then wound at intervals onto the shuttle. Beads can be placed so that they lie inside the ring, outside the ring like picots, or even across the ring, but they must always be put on the shuttle thread before commencing work. For beads inside a ring, the ring is made in the usual way and a bead is pushed along the shuttle thread when required. For beads decorating the outside of a ring, the required number of beads must be put onto the ring thread before starting to work the ring, and they are then slipped around the ring and held in place by the stitches on either side, which should be close to the bead. Beads lying across a ring are positioned after the ring has been completed and are held in place by joining to a picot. Shuttles which hold a large amount of thread are best when beads are to be put on the shuttle thread because the beads take up so much room. The American plastic shuttle from Boye is particularly useful for this kind of work.

The number of beads to be used on either the shuttle thread or the ball thread, or both, should be calculated so that the correct number of beads can be threaded to avoid joins in the work. Beads which are mounted on picots after the picot has been made are kept loose and are placed on the picot with the aid of a needle and thread as required. Loose beads may also be sewn onto a completed piece of work.

Transferring the beads onto the working threads

Generally the easiest way to put small beads onto the working thread is first to string the beads onto a fine thread (or keep them on the thread if they are pre-strung). Tie a loose overhand knot near the end of the *bead thread*, put the end of the working thread through this knot, and then pull the knot tight so that it holds the working thread securely. The required number of beads may then be gently pushed from the bead thread, over the knot, and onto the working thread.

BEADED CHRISTMAS TREE DECORATIONS

Glass beads are used on these decorations because they catch the light well as the decorations move. The beads are used on the chains on both decorations and so the required number of beads must be calculated and put on the ball thread before work commences.

Materials

No. 20 crochet thread in selected colour
20 small glass beads for the flower decoration
15 small glass beads for the star decoration

Measurements
Both decorations – $1\frac{3}{4}$in (4.3cm) diameter

Flower decoration

(Illustration 45)
In this decoration each of the five chains on the first round has one bead (five beads in all) and on the second round each chain has three beads (15 beads in all) – so a total of 20 beads must be put onto the ball thread. Wind sufficient thread onto the shuttle to make five rings and do not cut off from the ball.

1st round
1st ring: 10ds, l p, 10ds, cl. RW.
* *Chain:* 7ds, slide a bead along close to the last ds, 7ds. RW.
Next ring: 10ds, join to l p of 1st r, 10ds, cl. RW.

Rep from * until 5 rings have been made then rep the ch once more. Join the last ch to the 1st ch at the base of the 1st r and continue into the 2nd round.

2nd round
* *Chain:* 5ds, bead, 5ds, bead, 5ds, bead, 5ds, join to sp between the ch of the 1st round.

Rep from * 4 times. Cut the threads to 4in (10cm) and tie the ends together in an overhand knot to form a hanger. Damp the decoration, shape the chains evenly and leave to dry.

45 Beaded flower decoration

Star decoration

(Illustration 46)
In this decoration the five chains on both rounds are each decorated with one bead (ten beads in all). In addition a bead is placed between the chains of the second round and these five beads need to be put onto the ball thread together with the ten for the chains. Wind sufficient thread onto the shuttle to make five rings and do not cut off from the ball.

1st round
1st ring: 2ds, p, 2ds, p, 6ds, l p, 6ds, p, 2ds, p, 2ds, cl. RW.
* *Chain:* 7ds, bead, 7ds. RW.
Next ring: 2ds, p, 2ds, p, 6ds, join to l p of 1st r, 6ds, p, 2ds, p, 2ds, cl. RW.

Rep from * until 5 rings have been made, then rep the ch once more. Join the last ch to the 1st ch at the base of the 1st r, continue into the 2nd round.

2nd round
* *Chain:* 11ds, bead, 11ds, join to sp between ch of 1st round. Slide a bead along before starting the next ch.

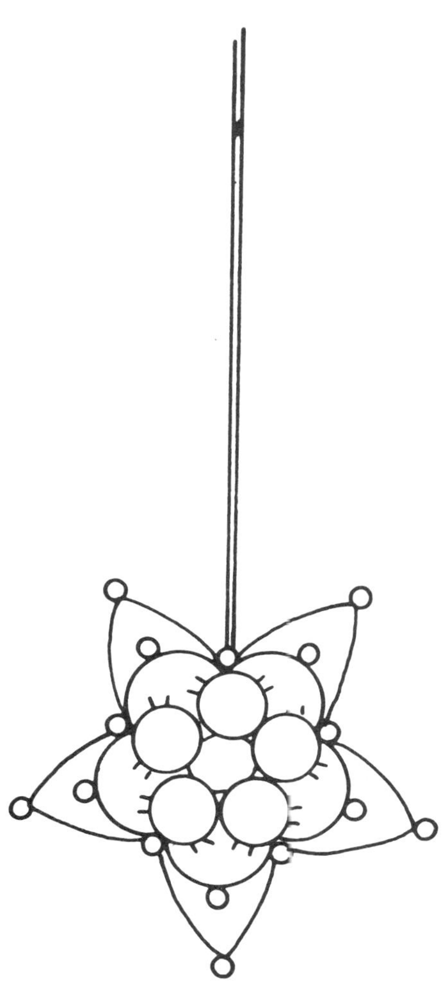

46 Beaded star decoration

47 Beaded daisy chain bracelet

Rep from * 4 times. Cut the working threads to 4in (10cm) and tie the ends together in an overhand knot to form a hanger. Damp the decoration, shape the chains to form points, pull out the picots and leave to dry.

DAISY CHAIN BRACELET

The beads on the bracelet lie on top of the centres of the tatted daisies. The required number of beads are put onto the shuttle thread and wound at intervals onto the shuttle. On completion of each ring a bead is taken along the shuttle thread, positioned on top of the ring and a join made in the picot opposite the start of the ring to hold the bead in place.

Materials

No. 20 crochet thread in white
18 gold beads, size P3
Piece of green velvet ribbon, 7in × $\frac{3}{8}$in (18cm × 1cm)
One small press stud

Measurements

Tatting – 6$\frac{3}{4}$in × $\frac{3}{8}$in (17cm × 1cm)
Completed bracelet – 7in × $\frac{3}{8}$in (18cm × 1cm)

48 A bead having been released from the shuttle about to be positioned on a ring on the daisy chain bracelet

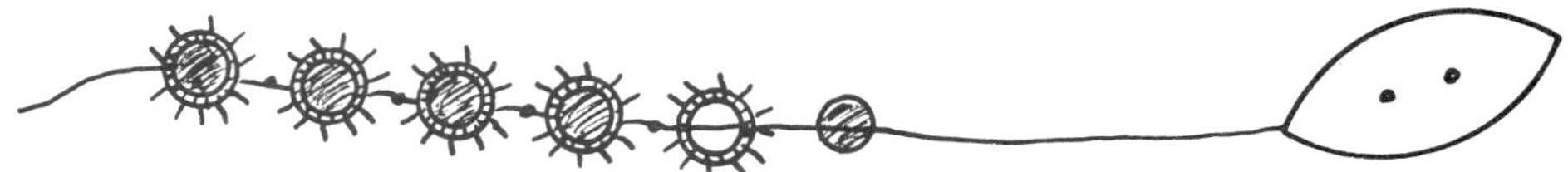

Daisy chain

Put the beads onto the working thread. Fill the shuttle, placing the beads at intervals along the thread on the shuttle. Cut off from the ball.

* *Ring:* 1ds, 11p sep by 1ds, 1ds, cl, slide a bead along the shuttle thread and position it on top of the ring just made (see Illustration 48). Secure the bead in this position by turning the work over and joining into the 6th p. Turn the work back again and leave a short piece of thread before starting the next r.

Rep from * until all the beads have been used, checking that the chain is the length required. Cut the thread.

To complete the bracelet

Damp the tatting, pull out the picots evenly and leave to dry. Cut the ends short and glue to the back. To prevent the velvet ribbon fraying put a little clear glue across the back of each end. Starting close to one end of the ribbon, glue the tatting centrally to it, leaving room at the end to sew on one half of the press stud. Sew the other half of the press stud to the back of the opposite end.

BEADED DRESS TRIM

The dress is decorated with one large and four small motifs. The small motif is composed of seven rings with a bead coming off each ring and in addition a bead is placed between each ring. All these beads must be put onto the working thread and wound

49 Dress trimmed with beaded motifs

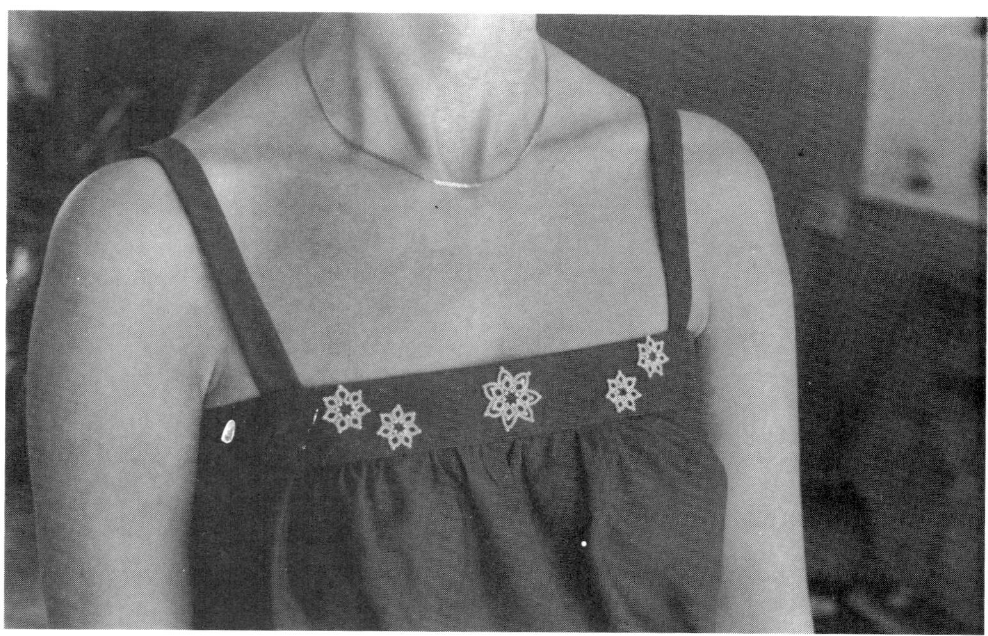

onto the shuttle before commencing work. The large motif has an additional round of chains, each decorated with a bead which is added from the ball thread.

Materials

No. 20 crochet thread in selected colour
For each small motif, 14 beads size P2
For each large motif, 21 beads size P2

Measurements

Small motif – 1in (2.5cm) diameter
Large motif – $1\frac{1}{2}$in (3.7cm) diameter

Small motif

Put 14 beads onto the working thread and wind onto the shuttle sufficient thread for seven rings, with the beads at intervals along it. Remember before starting each ring to slide a bead onto the ring thread ready to be incorporated into the ring. Only shuttle thread is used.

1st ring: leave 2in (5cm) thread at the start. Put a bead on the ring thread, 3ds, p, 3ds, slide the bead around the ring so that it lies close to the last stitch made, 3ds, p, 3ds, cl.

* Slide a bead to the base of the previous r, so that it will lie in the space between the rings.

Next ring: work this close to the last bead. Put a bead on the ring thread, 3ds, join to last p of previous r, 3ds, slide the bead around the ring close to the last stitch made, 3ds, p, 3ds, cl.

Rep from * until 6 rings have been made then slide a bead to the base of the previous r.

7th ring: put a bead on the ring thread. 3ds, join to last p of previous r, 3ds, slide the bead in place, 3ds, join to 1st p of 1st r, 3ds, cl. Slide the last bead close to the base of the last r.

Tie the ends together in a neat knot, cut and finish off neatly.

Large motif

Work a small motif.

Put seven beads onto the working thread, wind a small amount of thread onto the shuttle and do not cut off from the ball.

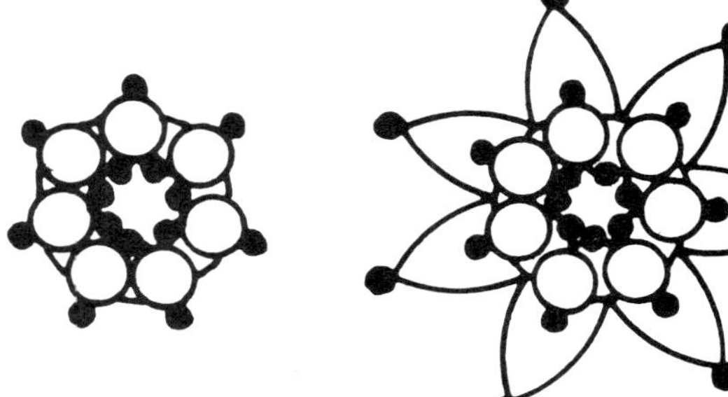

50 Diagram showing the construction details of two sizes of beaded motifs

Join to a picot which joins two rings together on the small motif.

* *Chain:* 6ds, slide a bead along from the ball thread, 6ds, join to the next p which joins two rings together on the small motif.

Rep from * 6 times, join to the same p used at the beg of the round.

Tie ends, cut and finish off neatly.

To attach the motifs

Position the motifs. With a needle and thread catch the small motifs in place through the picots used for joining the rings together. The large motifs can be attached in the same way and a stitch may also be put through the thread near the beads on the chains.

BEADED BRAID

This braid is useful for adding a festive touch to the collars, cuffs and pockets of plain clothes. The braid is composed of rings and chains with a bead between each ring and each chain. The beads to be placed between the rings are not put on the working thread because they are put on very long picots which come off the rings, and the same long picots are used for joining the rings together. The beads required for placing between the chains are put on the ball thread before work commences.

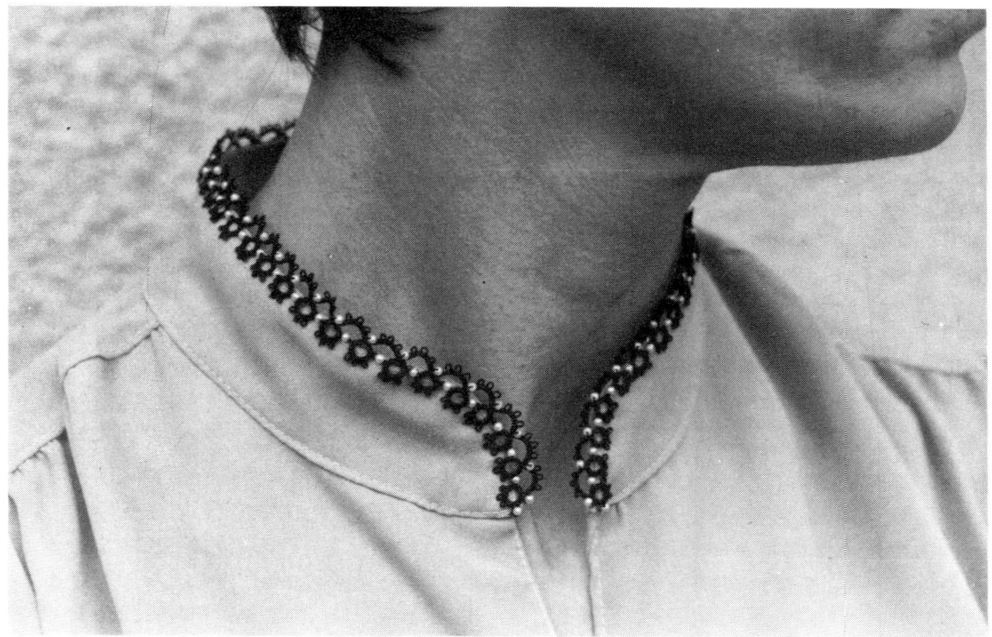

51 Braid with beads between the rings and the chains

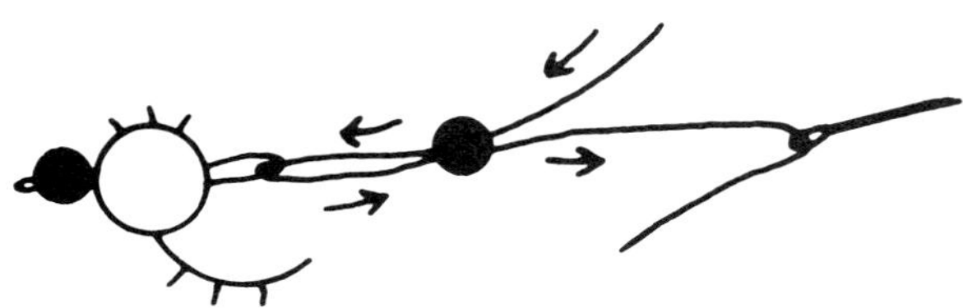

52 Mounting a bead on a picot, using a needle and thread. The arrows show the movement of the needle and thread

53 Detail of the beaded braid

Materials

No. 40 crochet thread in selected colour
Six beads for each 1in (2.5cm) braid, size P2
Spacer, $\frac{3}{10}$in (8mm) wide, for measuring the long picots
Fine needle and 6in (15cm) sewing thread

Measurements

Approximately three rings and three chains to 1in (2.5cm)
$\frac{1}{2}$in (12mm) wide

Mounting beads on picots

The bead is quite easily put on the picot using the needle and sewing thread. Put the needle and thread through the bead, then through the picot and back through the opposite side of the bead (Illustration 52). Hold the two ends of the thread together and carefully slide the bead from the sewing thread onto the picot. Remove the needle and thread.

The braid

For each 1in (2.5cm) of braid required, put three beads onto the working thread. Wind the necessary amount of thread onto the shuttle and do not cut off from the ball.

1st ring: 3ds, l p, 3ds, 3p sep by 2ds, 3ds, l p, 3ds, cl. RW.

* *Chain:* slide a bead along, 3ds, 3p sep by 2ds, 3ds. RW.

Ring: 3ds, put a bead on the l p of the previous r, then join to this p, 3ds, 3p sep by

2ds, 3ds, l p, 3ds, cl. RW.

Rep from * to the length required. Tie ends and cut.

To finish

Sew all the ends down securely. Damp the work, shape the chains, pull out the picots and flatten the braid. Leave to dry. Catch the braid in place through the centre picot of each ring, either to the edge of the fabric or so that the whole ring is on the fabric. Add a bead to the long picot on the first and last rings.

MOBILE MEDALLIONS WITH SEQUIN CENTRES

The tatting on these mobile medallions is worked round a sequin and as the mobile moves the light catches the sequins and makes them sparkle. Wheel sequins are used; these are ½in (12mm) in diameter with eight holes evenly spaced round the scalloped edge. They come in a variety of colours so the mobile can be made with sequins all of one colour or with mixed colours. The tatting is joined to the holes in the sequin in the same way as joining to a picot. The medallions can be used for purposes other than a mobile. The size can be adjusted by working in different threads or by slightly adapting the patterns as shown in the instructions for the handbag mirror medallion.

Working with sequins

Perspiration from the hands, water and spray starch will damage or remove the metallic finish of the sequins so, in order to protect the surface, carefully cover each side with clear nail varnish and allow it to dry thoroughly before beginning work. When joining the tatting to the sequins gently manoeuvre the thread so that the join is neat but avoid pulling the thread too tight or the sequin may break.

Alternative to sequin centre

(Illustration 55B)

If difficulty is experienced either in working

54 A mobile with medallions of tatting worked around sequin centres

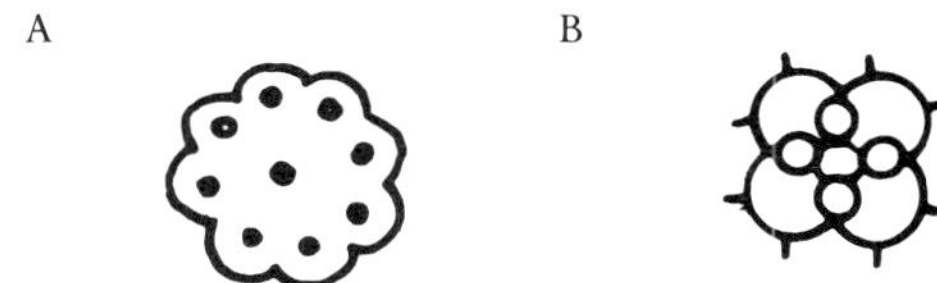

55 A diagram of a wheel sequin and the tatted centre which can be used in place of the sequin in the mobile medallions

with the sequins or in obtaining them they can be replaced with a tatted centre where the picots on the outer chains replace the holes around the sequin. The tatted centre can be made in a different shade if desired.

Tatted centre

Using No. 60 crochet thread:

1st ring: 5ds, l p, 5ds, cl. RW.

1st chain: 3ds, p, 4ds, p, 3ds. RW.

* *Next ring:* 5ds, join to the l p of the 1st r, 5ds, cl. RW.

Next chain: as 1st ch.

Rep from * twice, join the last ch to the 1st ch at the base of the 1st r. Tie ends and cut short. Glue ends neatly to one side.

The medallions

Materials

No. 60 crochet thread in selected colour
Five wheel sequins coated with nail varnish
Two shuttles
Two pieces 1mm diameter wire, 10½in (26cm) and 7in (17.5cm) long

Measurements

Medallions 1, 2, 4, 5 – 2in (5cm)
Medallion 3 – 2½in (6.2cm)

Medallion 1

(Illustration 56)

This medallion is worked entirely of chains. Wind a small amount of thread onto the shuttle and join the thread into a hole in the sequin in the same way as joining to a picot.

1st round: * *chain:* sm p, 10ds, join to next hole in sequin. Rep from * all round the sequin, joining the last ch to the sm p made at the beg of the 1st ch. Continue without breaking the thread into:

2nd round: * *chain:* sm p, 14ds, join to the sm p of the ch below. Rep from * all round, join the last ch to the 1st sm p of this round. Continue into:

3rd round: * *chain:* sm p, 3ds, 5p sep by 3ds, 3ds, join to the sm p of the ch below. Rep from * joining the last ch to the 1st ch as before. Continue into:

4th round: * *chain:* sm p, 3ds, 7 p sep by 3ds, 3ds, join to sm p of ch below. Rep from * all round, join last ch to 1st ch as before.

Tie ends and cut, leaving 10in (25cm) thread for hanging.

Medallion 2

(Illustration 57)

This medallion is worked with two shuttles. Half fill one shuttle, unwind a similar amount from the ball and wind onto the second shuttle to avoid a join at the start.

1st round:

* *Ring:* 2ds, 3p sep by 2ds, 2ds, join to a hole in the sequin, 2ds, 3p sep by 2ds, 2ds, cl. RW.
Chain: 2ds, 7p sep by 2ds, 2ds. RW.

Rep from * all round the sequin, join the last ch to the 1st ch at the base of the 1st r. Continue without breaking the thread into:

2nd round:

* *Chain:* 2ds, 5p sep by 2ds, 2ds. With the second shuttle work the *small ring:* 1ds, 7p sep by 1ds, 1ds, cl. With the first shuttle complete the chain, 2ds, 5p sep by 2ds, 2ds, join to the sp between the ch on the 1st round.

Rep from * all round. Tie ends and cut leaving 10in (25cm) thread for hanging.

Medallion 3

(Illustration 58)

* *1st ring:* 7ds, join to a hole in the sequin, 7ds, cl. RW.
1st chain: 7ds. RW.
2nd ring: 1ds, 3p sep by 5ds, 5ds, cl. RW.

The following three chains are worked in a clockwise direction around the 2nd ring and each chain joins into a picot on the ring.

2nd chain: 8ds, 4p sep by 2ds, 2ds, join to the nearest p on the previous r. *N.B.* On repeats work instead: 8ds, join to last p of previous 4th ch, 2ds, 3p sep by 2ds, 2ds, join to p on

56 Mobile medallion 1

57 Mobile medallion 2

58 Mobile medallion 3

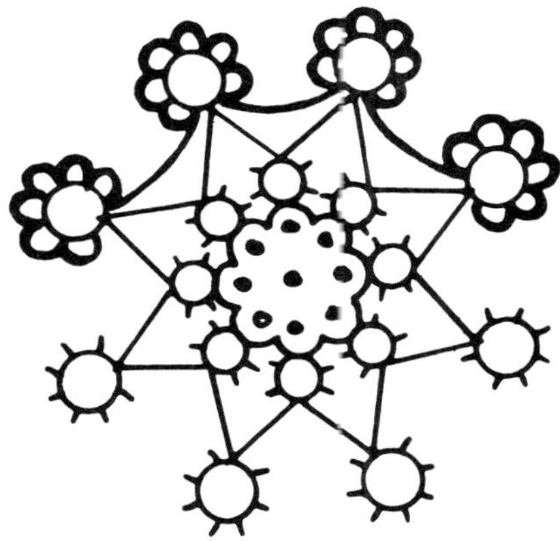

59 Mobile medallion 4

previous r.
3rd chain: 2ds, 7p sep by 2ds, 2ds, join to next p on previous r.
4th chain: 2ds, 4p sep by 2ds, 8ds, join to next p on previous r.
5th chain: 7ds. RW.

Rep from * all round the sequin remembering on the last rep to join the last p of the 4th ch to the 1st p of the first 2nd ch made at the beg of the round. Join the last ch to the 1st ch at the base of the 1st r.

Tie ends and cut short. Cut a 12in (30cm) length of thread and tie it to a picot joining a 2nd and 4th ch, having one end 10in (25cm) long, knot firmly and cut the other end short.

Medallion 4

(Illustration 59)
This medallion is constructed by working rings around the sequin alternately with larger rings separated by ¼in (6mm) thread; it is helpful to measure this thread using a spacer. On the 2nd round chains are worked around the larger rings. The diagram has been left incomplete to show the construction more clearly.
1st round: using shuttle thread only:
* *Ring:* 3ds, 2p sep by 3ds, 3ds, join to a hole in the sequin, 3ds, 2p sep by 3ds, 3ds, cl. RW. Leave ¼in (6mm) thread.
Ring: 3ds, 7p sep by 3ds, 3ds, cl. RW. Leave ¼in (6mm) thread.

Rep from * all round the sequin, finishing by leaving ¼in (6mm) thread and tying the threads close to the base of the 1st r made. Cut the thread.
2nd round: using ball and shuttle thread, the chains are worked clockwise around the large outer rings, joining in turn to the picots of these rings. Join to the first p on the left-hand side of a large r.
** *Chain:* * 5ds, join to next p on r, rep from * five times.
Chain: 8ds, join to first p on the left-hand side of the next large r.

Rep from ** 7 times. Tie ends and cut short.

Cut a 12in (30cm) length of thread and tie it to the centre picot of any large ring, having one end 10in (25cm) long, knot firmly and cut the other end short.

Medallion 5

(Illustration 60)
The 1st round of this medallion is composed of rings and chains, the chains being joined to the sequin. On the 2nd round, large rings join to the side picots of the rings of the 1st round and small rings join to the centre picots, and both are separated by chains. The diagram has been left incomplete to show the construction more clearly.
1st round:
* *Ring:* 4ds, 3p sep by 4ds, 4ds, cl. RW.
Chain: 7ds, join to hole in sequin, 7ds. RW.

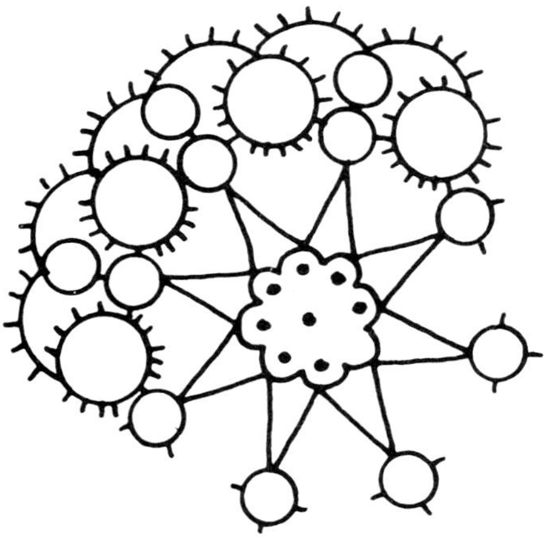

60 Mobile medallion 5

Rep from * all round the sequin, join the last ch to the 1st ch at the base of the 1st r. Tie ends and cut short.

2nd round:

* *Large ring:* 2ds, 4p sep by 2ds, 2ds, join to the side p of a r on the 1st round, 2ds, 5p sep by 2ds, 2ds, join to the side p of the next r on the 1st round, 2ds, 4p sep by 2ds, 2ds, cl. RW.
1st chain: 2ds, 5p sep by 2ds, 2ds. RW.
Small ring: 7ds, join to the centre p of the same r on the 1st round as previous r was joined to, 7ds, cl. RW.
2nd chain: as 1st ch.

Rep from * all round the 1st round, join the last ch to the 1st ch at the base of the 1st r. Tie ends and cut, leaving 10in (25cm) thread for hanging.

To complete the medallions

Secure all the short ends to one side with glue. Damp and shape the medallions then pin them out so that they are as flat as possible. Leave to dry.

To make up the mobile

Use these instructions with Illustration 54.

1. Turn over ½in (12mm) on each end of each wire to form hooks.
2. Attach the two medallions on the ends of the short wire and position the hanging thread (approximately 5in (12.5cm) long) so that this wire balances. Then seal the knots with a touch of glue or clear nail varnish and cut the ends short.
3. Suspend this balanced wire and the remaining medallions on the longer wire as shown – the position of the hanging threads is not critical to approximately ½in (12mm), since the final adjustment for the overall balance of the mobile is achieved by adjusting the position of the main hanging thread. Seal the knots as before.

4 Gifts

HANDBAG MIRROR MEDALLION

The medallion shown in illustration 61 was worked from the pattern for the mobile medallion No. 5, but the alternative tatted centre was used instead of a sequin and it was made slightly larger by adding a round of chains. The original was worked in two colours, white and yellow, and looks very effective so the instructions are given with details of the colour positions.

Materials

No. 60 crochet thread in white and yellow
Handbag mirror, 3in (7.5cm) diameter, with a recess for holding lace

Measurement

2½in (6.2cm) diameter

The medallion

Centre
Using yellow thread for both rings and chains, make an alternative tatted centre from the instructions given at the beginning of the mobile pattern.

1st round
Using yellow thread in the shuttle for the rings and a ball of white thread for the chains, complete this round as given for the mobile medallion, joining into the picots of the centre in place of the holes in the sequin.

61 A medallion mounted in the frame of a handbag mirror

2nd round
Using white thread in the shuttle for the rings and a ball of yellow thread for the chains, complete this round as given for the mobile medallion. Tie the ends and cut short.

3rd round
Wind a small amount of yellow thread onto the shuttle and do not cut off from the ball. Join to the centre picot of any chain on the previous round.
* *Chain:* 2ds, 7p sep by 2ds, 2ds, join to the centre p of the next ch on the previous round. Rep from * all round. Tie ends and cut short.

To complete
Glue all ends neatly to one side. Damp the work and pull into shape, taking care that

the medallion is circular because any significant unevenness will show when the work is mounted in the frame.

LAVENDER BAG

The lavender bag is trimmed with a tatted edging, motif and pearls. The edging is constructed of rings only, but the work is reversed and an even amount of thread left before each ring is made. The amount of thread between the rings can be measured accurately by using a spacer. The motif is made in a similar way. The pearls are added to both the edging and the motif after the lace has been sewn onto the made-up bag. If a simpler effect is desired then the motif and the pearls can be omitted. It is best to make up the lavender bag first so that the correct amount of edging is made and can be fitted on evenly.

62 A lavender bag decorated with an edging and motif of tatted rings and pearls

Materials

Piece of fine material, 5in × 9in (12.5cm × 22.5cm)
Lavender, or a mixture of lavender and soft stuffing
No. 40 crochet thread
⅕in (5mm) spacer
Approximately 30 pearls, size P2
6in × ¼in (15cm × 6mm) ribbon for hanging

Measurements

Bag and lace – approximately 3¾in × 3¼in (9.3cm × 8.1cm)
Lace edging – ½in (12mm) wide
Motif – 1½in (3.7cm) diameter

To make the bag

1. Make a paper pattern of the heart by clipping a thin sheet of paper or tracing paper on top of Illustration 63, tracing round the shape and marking the dots.
2. Cut out the tracing, pin it on to a doubled piece of material (right sides together) and cut out. Mark the dots on the material.
3. Leaving a gap between the dots, sew a ¼in (6mm) seam. Clip the curves and turn to the right side. Press the bag flat with the open seam allowance underneath.
4. Fill the bag with lavender or a mixture of lavender and stuffing and sew up the hole neatly.

The edging

This is worked with shuttle thread only.
* *Inner ring:* 6ds, p, 6ds, cl. RW. Leave ⅕in (5mm) thread.
Outer ring: 2ds, 6p sep by 2ds, 2ds, cl. RW. Leave ⅕in (5mm) thread.

Rep from * until 24 inner and 23 outer rings have been made. Before cutting the thread check that this length will fit neatly

63 Pattern for the lavender bag

round the bag by pinning the picots of the inner rings to the bag so that these rings lie on the bag and the outer rings stand off the edge. Adjust the length if necessary.

The motif

This is worked with shuttle thread only. Leave 4in (10cm) thread at the start.

1st inner ring: 4ds, p, 2ds, p, 4ds, cl. RW. Leave $\frac{1}{5}$in (5mm) thread.

* *Outer ring:* 2ds, 6p sep by 2ds, 2ds, cl. RW. Leave $\frac{1}{5}$in (5mm) thread.

Next inner ring: 4ds, join to the last p of the previous inner r, 2ds, p, 4ds, cl. RW. Leave $\frac{1}{5}$in (5mm) thread.

Rep from * until 5 inner and outer rings have been made.

Last inner ring: 4ds, join to the last p of the previous inner r, 2ds, join to the first p of the 1st inner r, 4ds, cl. RW. Leave $\frac{1}{5}$in (5mm) thread.

Last outer ring: as previous outer r.

Join the working thread and the thread left at the beginning of the 1st ring into a tight knot close to the last outer ring, taking care to leave the same amount of thread as before between these two rings. Cut the threads.

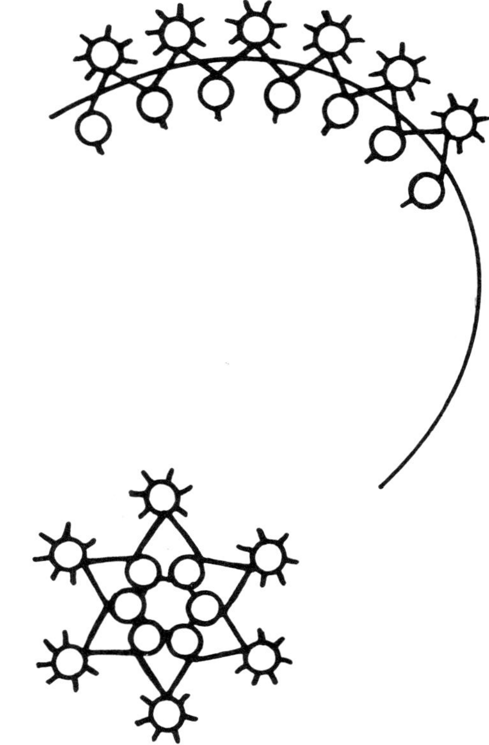

64 Diagram showing construction details of the lavender bag edging and motif

To complete

Sew or glue all ends to one side. Sew the edging onto the bag through the picots of the inner rings and also at the base of these rings. Sew a pearl over each inner ring picot. Sew the motif to the centre of the bag. Sew a pearl between each inner ring, over the picots used for joining, taking care to make a neat circle of pearls. Fold the ribbon in half and sew it neatly to the top of the bag to form a loop for hanging.

65 Small paperweight worked in two colours

PAPERWEIGHTS

Glass paperweights, with a recess deep enough for holding lace, are available in various shapes and a range of sizes. Some paperweights magnify significantly so that every detail shows, as well as making the lace appear coarser than it actually is. The round and square paperweights used in the following two projects magnify only very slightly but since they are showpieces care must be taken to work and join evenly. Ends should be finished as unobtrusively as possible by being glued to one side. The simplest way to hold the lace in place and to back the paperweight is to use Fablon Velour, which is available in several colours. The felt side is used outside the paperweight and the sticky side is used as a backing for the lace.

To make up a paperweight

1. Draw carefully round the paperweight onto the backing paper of the Fablon Velour and cut out, slightly inside the marking, with small scissors.
2. Peel off the backing paper and place the tatted motif centrally onto the sticky side.
3. Place the paperweight centrally on top of the motif.
4. After checking that the motif is evenly positioned in the paperweight, press the Fablon firmly to the back and trim off any excess neatly.

Round paperweight motif

This pattern for a small round paperweight is worked in a No. 60 crochet thread. It looks well when the centre motif is worked in a colour contrasting with that used for the edging.

Materials

No. 60 crochet thread in two colours
$2\frac{1}{2}$in (6.2cm) diameter glass paperweight with a recess for holding lace
$2\frac{1}{2}$in (6.2cm) diameter piece of Fablon Velour for the backing, in a colour contrasting to the threads

Measurement

Motif – 2in (5cm) diameter

Centre motif

This is made using the first colour.
1st ring: 2ds, 5p sep by 2ds, 2ds, cl. RW.
1st chain: 2ds, 5p sep by 2ds, 2ds. RW.
* *Next ring:* 2ds, p, 2ds, join to 4th p of previous r, 2ds, 3p sep by 2ds, 2ds, cl. RW.
Next chain: as 1st ch.
Rep from * twice.
5th ring: 2ds, p, 2ds, join to 4th p of previous r, 2ds, p, 2ds, join to 2nd p of 1st r, 2ds, p, 2ds, cl. RW.
5th chain: As 1st ch, join to the 1st ch at the base of the 1st r.
Tie ends and cut short.

Edging
This is made using the second colour.
1st ring: 3ds, 3p sep by 3ds, 3ds, cl.
2nd ring: 3ds, join to last p of previous r, 2ds, 6p sep by 2ds, 3ds, cl.
3rd ring: 3ds, join to last p of previous r, 3ds, 2p sep by 3ds, 3ds, cl. RW.
1st chain: 3ds, p, 6ds, join to 2nd p of any ch of the centre motif, 6ds, p, 3ds. RW.
* *4th ring:* 3ds, p, 3ds, join to centre p of previous r, 3ds, p, 3ds, cl.
5th ring: 3ds, join to last p of previous r, 2ds, 6p sep by 2ds, 3ds, cl.
6th ring: 3ds, join to last p of previous r, 3ds, 2p sep by 3ds, 3ds, cl. RW.
Next chain: 3ds, join to adjacent p of previous ch, 6ds, join to 4th p of the same ch of the centre motif as was used before, 6ds, p, 3ds. RW.

Rep rings 4, 5 and 6.
Next chain: 3ds, join to adjacent p of previous ch, 6ds, join to 2nd p of next ch of centre motif, 6ds, p, 3ds. RW.

Rep from * 4 times but making the last ring of the final clover and the last chain as follows:
Last ring: 3ds, join to last p of previous r, 3ds, join to 2nd p of 1st r made, 3ds, p, 3ds, cl. RW.
Last chain: 3ds, join to adjacent p of previous ch, 6ds, join to 4th p of ch on centre motif, 6ds, join to 1st p of 1st ch made, 3ds, join to base of 1st r made. Tie ends and cut short.

To complete the paperweight
Glue all the ends neatly to one side. Damp the motif, shape the chains and picots evenly and ensure that the motif is circular, because any significant unevenness will be noticeable when the work is mounted in the paperweight. Leave to dry. Make up the paperweight as described earlier.

Square paperweight motif
This motif, worked in a No. 40 crochet thread, is made up of a centre square, worked with two shuttles, and an edging worked round the square so that the corners of the square face the sides of the edging.

66 Square paperweight

Materials
No. 40 crochet thread in selected colour
Two shuttles
$2\frac{1}{2}$in (6.2cm) square paperweight with a recess for holding lace
$2\frac{1}{2}$in (6.2cm) square of Fablon Velour in a contrasting colour

Measurements
Centre square – $1\frac{1}{8}$in (2.9cm) square
Complete motif – $1\frac{7}{8}$in (4.8cm) square

Centre square
(Illustration 67)
Half fill two shuttles with an unbroken thread.
1st large corner ring: 3ds, 6p sep by 3ds, 3ds, cl. RW.
* *Chain:* 2ds. RW.
Ring: 3ds, join to last p of previous r, 3ds, 3p sep by 3ds, 6ds, cl. RW.
Chain: 4ds. Then, with 2nd shuttle:
Small centre ring: 4ds, p long enough to join the next 3 centre rings into, 4ds, cl.

With 1st shuttle complete the chain, 4ds. RW.
Ring: 6ds, join to the last p of the ring made before the small centre r, 3ds, 3p sep by 3ds, 3ds, cl. RW.
Chain: 2ds. RW.
Large corner ring: 3ds, join to last p of

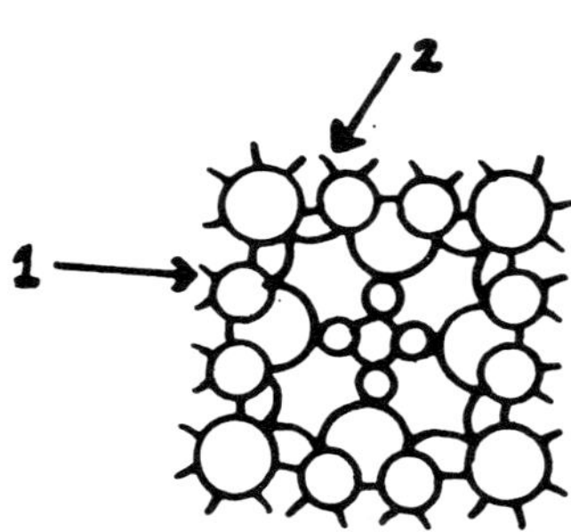

67 Centre square of paperweight motif. Arrow 1 indicates the picot used for the 1st join on the edging, and arrow 2 the picot used for the second join on the edging

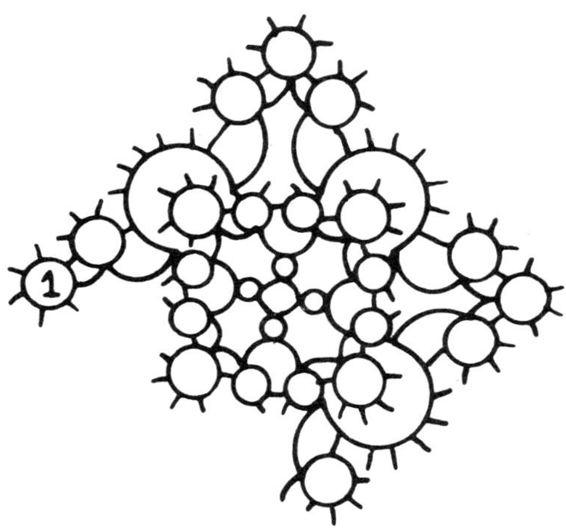

68 Diagram showing how the edging joins the centre square

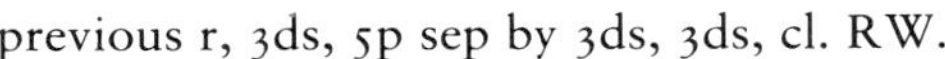

previous r, 3ds, 5p sep by 3ds, 3ds, cl. RW.

Rep from * (joining all the small centre rings to the picot of the 1st centre ring), until the 4th corner is about to be completed, then work the last ring and chain as follows:

Last ring: 6ds, join to last p of previous r, 3ds, 2p sep by 3ds, 3ds, join to 1st p of 1st large corner r, 3ds, cl. RW.

Last chain: 2ds, join to base of 1st r. Tie ends and cut short.

Edging

(Illustrations 67 and 68)

Large ring: (ring marked 1 on Illustration 68) 3ds, 6p sep by 3ds, 3ds, cl. RW.

* *Chain:* 2ds. RW.

Ring: 3ds, join to last p of previous r, 3ds, 4p sep by 3ds, 3ds cl. RW.

Chain: 5ds, join to the centre square at the p arrowed and numbered 1 in Illustration 67, RW, and working over the large corner r of the centre continue the ch, 3ds, join to last p of previous r, 3ds, 6p sep by 3ds, 3ds, join to the centre square at the p arrowed and numbered 2 in Illustration 67, RW and complete the ch with 5ds. RW.

Ring: 3ds, join to last p of last ch, 3ds, 4p sep by 3ds, 3ds cl. RW.

Chain: 2ds. RW.

Large ring: 3ds, join to last p of previous r, 3ds, 5p sep by 3ds, 3ds, cl. RW.

Rep from * 3 times, omitting the large ring on the last repeat and making the last ring and chain as follows:

Last ring: 3ds, join to last p of previous ch, 3ds, 3p sep by 3ds, 3ds, join to 1st p of 1st large r, 3ds, cl. RW.

Last chain: 2ds, join to base of 1st r made. Tie ends and cut short.

To complete the paperweight

Glue all ends neatly to one side. Damp the motif and shape, particularly the outer chains. Pin the motif to the measurements given, making it as square as possible. Leave to dry. Make up the paperweight as described earlier.

CUSHION (OR TOWEL) DECORATIONS

The strip of lace and the motifs decorating the cushion are worked in a No. 20 crochet thread which produces a bold look in the tatting. For a more delicate effect, to decorate clothing for example, simply use a finer thread. The strip of lace is made by first working the centre rings and one side to the length required, after which the second side is worked.

69 Cushion decorated with a strip of lace and matching medallions (*opposite*)

Materials

No. 20 crochet thread in selected colour
Cushion, 16in (40cm) square

Measurements

Depth of lace – $2\frac{3}{4}$in (6.8cm)
Length of lace – $22\frac{1}{2}$in (56cm)
Small medallion – $2\frac{3}{4}$in (6.8cm) diameter
Larger medallion – $3\frac{1}{4}$in (8cm) diameter

Strip of lace

(Illustration 70)

First side

* *Centre ring:* 2ds, 11p sep by 2ds, 2ds, cl. RW.
Chain A: 10ds. RW.
Outer ring: the outer rings have ten picots, five of which are used later for joining the chains surrounding these rings, so they should be quite small; the other five picots alternating with them are for decoration and should be larger. 1ds, sm p, 2ds, larger p, 2ds, then 8p which are alternately small and larger, sep by 2ds, 2ds, cl. RW.

The next five chains are worked round the reversed ring in a clockwise direction, joining to each of the small picots of the ring in turn.
Chain 1: 10ds, join to next sm p of previous r.
Chain 2: 5ds, p, 5ds, join to next sm p. *N.B.* When repeating the pattern work: 5ds, join to p of chain 4 of the previous set of chains, 5ds, join to next sm p.
Chain 3: 5ds, 3p sep by 1ds, 5ds, join to next sm p.
Chain 4: 5ds, p, 5ds, join to next sm p.
Chain 5: 9ds, join to next sm p.
Chain B: 10ds. RW.

Rep from * to the length required, ending with a centre ring. The two centre rings at the beginning and end fit into the corners of the cushion. Tie ends and cut.

Second side

On the second side no centre rings are made, the edging being joined to the 6th picot of the centre rings of the first side. See Illustration 70. Join to the 6th p of the last centre ring and work the pattern from chain A to chain B, joining chain B to the 6th p of the next centre ring, and then without reversing continue straight into chain A. Continue until the last centre ring is attached. Tie ends and cut.

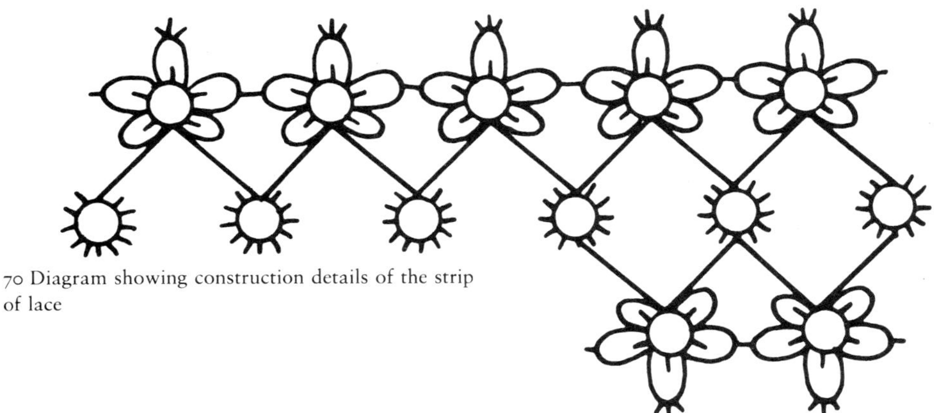

70 Diagram showing construction details of the strip of lace

71 Diagram showing construction details of the medallions

Matching medallions

(Illustration 71)

Make two small medallions and one larger one. The instructions for the larger medallion are given in brackets.

Centre ring: * 2ds, p, 2ds, sm p, rep from * 4 times, 2ds, p, 2ds – producing 5 sm p and 6p – cl, form a 6th sm p by leaving a small sp and tying the ball and shuttle threads in a tight knot. RW.

** *Chain A:* 8(10)ds. RW.

Outer ring: 1ds, sm p, 2ds, p, 2ds, 8p – alternately sm and larger – sep by 2ds, 2ds, cl. RW.

Outer chains are worked round the outer ring and joined to the small picots of the outer ring.

Chain 1: 8(10)ds, join to next sm p on outer r.

Chain 2: as chain 1.

Chain 3: 4(5)ds, 3p sep by 1ds, 4(5)ds, join to next sm p.

Chain 4: as chain 1.

Chain 5: 7(9)ds, join to next sm p.

Chain B: 8(10)ds, join to next sm p on centre r.

Rep from ** 5 times, join the last ch to the sm p made by tying the threads together. Tie ends and cut.

To complete the cushion

Sew all ends neatly to one side. Damp and shape the work. Stretch and pin out the strip of lace so that it dries to the required measurement. Pin the points of the medallions so that they dry evenly spaced. Starch and leave to dry thoroughly. Sew the strip of lace diagonally across the cushion. Sew the larger medallion 2in (5cm) from another corner and the two small medallions in the remaining space on that side, parallel to the strip of lace.

Towel decoration

The pattern for the strip of lace and the medallions on the decorated cushion can be used effectively for towels. A strip of lace can be attached as an edging or it can be applied to the end panel of the towel where it will

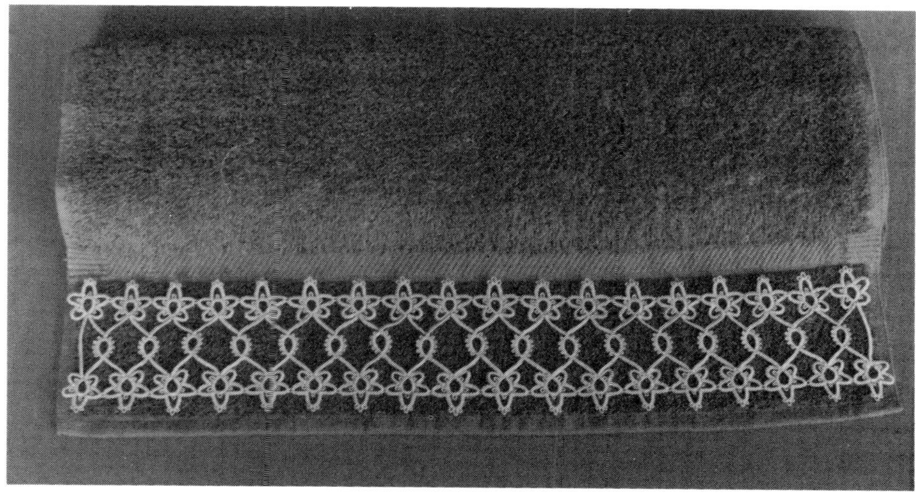

72 A towel with a strip of lace applied to the end panel

73 Three medallions decorating the end panel of a towel

show to advantage during use (Illustration 72). Three small medallions applied to the end panel are an alternative decoration (illustration 73).

The materials and measurements of the lace are the same as for the lace on the decorated cushion.

First side

Following the pattern for the decorated cushion, *start with the outer ring* and work the length required, ending (but not cutting the threads) after chain 5.

Next chain: 23ds. RW. Continue into the second side.

Second side

Start the pattern at the outer ring and complete this side with a *final chain* of 23ds. Join to the space at the base of the 1st outer ring on the first side. Tie ends and cut.

To complete the towel

Finish the lace as instructed for the cushion and sew to the towel as desired.

74 Tatted picture frame

ROUND PICTURE FRAME

A tatted, beaded braid with an edging on one side frames the small picture. The tatting and the picture are mounted onto a piece of covered card which can be made to stand or hang. Alternatively, a set of pictures look attractive put on a length of ribbon. The size of the frame can be altered simply by adjusting the length of the beaded braid.

Materials

No. 40 crochet thread in black or selected colour
11 silver oval beads, size P01
Small picture, size approximately 1½in (3.7cm) diameter, but do not cut until the tatting is complete
Two pieces of stiff card approximately 2½in (6.2cm) diameter (prepare when the tatting is complete)
Piece of material 3½in (8.7cm) diameter to cover the card

Measurements

Finished frame – 2½in (6.2cm) diameter
Tatting – ½in (12mm) wide

Beaded braid

(Illustration 75)
Put all the beads onto the working thread, then wind some thread onto the shuttle adding the beads at intervals. Cut off from the ball. Leave 1½in (3.7cm) thread at the start.

* *Ring:* 3ds, 4p sep by 3ds, 6ds, p, 6ds, cl. Slide a bead along the shuttle thread to lie across the r, join to 4th p to secure the bead.

Rep from * until all the beads have been used. Tie the shuttle thread and the length of thread left at the beginning of the work into a tight knot close to the start of the 1st ring. Cut the ends short.

Edging

The edging is worked with ball and shuttle thread along one side of the beaded braid, joining into the picots between the two sets of six double stitches.
1st ring: 4ds, join to any outside p on the braid, 4ds, cl. RW.
* *Chain:* 8ds. RW.
Ring: 4ds, join to same p as previous r, 4ds, cl. RW.
Chain: 10ds. RW.
Ring: 4ds, join to next outside p of braid, 4ds, cl. RW.

Rep from * around the braid omitting the last ring on the final rep, then join the final ch of 10ds to the 1st ch at the base of the 1st r. Tie ends and cut short.

To complete the frame

Glue all the ends to one side. Damp the tatting, pull out the picots, shape the chains

75 Diagram showing the construction of the picture frame

evenly and ensure that the work is circular before leaving to dry.

Cut two pieces of card the same diameter as the finished piece of tatting, and a piece of material 1in (2.5cm) larger than the card. With a needle and a length of sewing thread make small running stitches ¼in (6mm) from the edge of the material, place one piece of card in the centre and pull up the thread so that the material fits tightly. Fasten off the thread securely.

Cut the picture to a size to fit neatly inside the tatted frame, with the edge under the beaded braid. Glue the picture to the centre of the covered card and then carefully glue the tatting around the picture. Glue the second piece of card to the back of the frame.

To make a hanger, glue a small piece of folded ribbon to the back at the top centre. To make the frame free standing, cut a strip of card ½in × 1½in (12mm × 3.7cm), glue the end third of this strip and stick it to the back of the frame in the centre. Bend the strip to support the frame.

76 Pictures mounted on a piece of ribbon

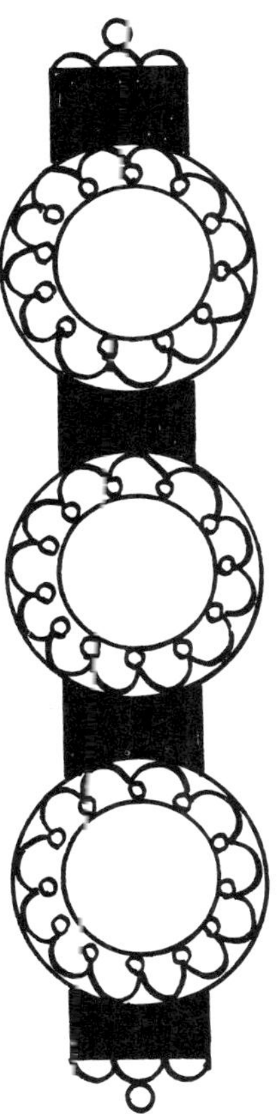

TRINKET BOX DECORATION

The motif in the lid of the box was worked in two colours, pink and white. Two shuttles are used in the construction of the centre motif and the 1st round.

Materials

No. 60 crochet thread in two colours
Trinket box, 3in (7.5cm) diameter, with a lid designed for holding lace
Piece of backing material, 3in (7.5cm) diameter

Measurement

2½in (6.2cm) diameter

Centre motif

Half fill two shuttles in the two different colour threads. Start with the shuttle holding the thread of the colour required for the centre group of rings.
1st ring: using shuttle 1, 3ds, 5p sep by 3ds, 3ds, cl. RW.
1st chain: using thread from shuttle 2 as the ball thread, 3ds, 5p sep by 2ds, 3ds. RW.
* *Ring:* 3ds, p, 3ds, join to 4th p of previous r,

77 A trinket box with a motif mounted in the lid

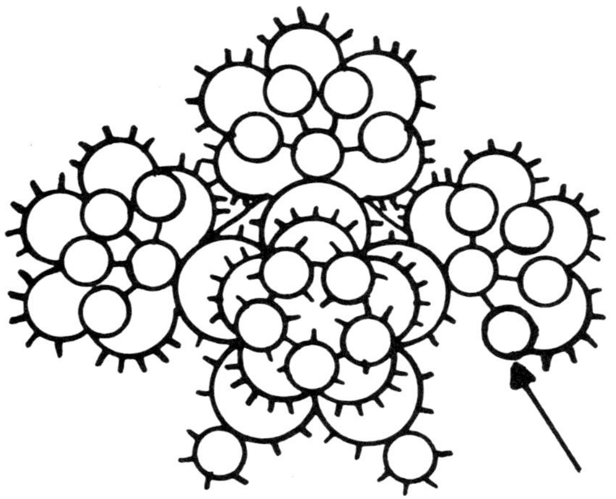

78 Diagram showing the construction of the motif used in the trinket box and for the brooch (next chapter)

3ds, 3p sep by 3ds, 3ds, cl. RW.
Chain: as 1st ch.

Rep from * until 4 rings and chains have been made.

5th ring: 3ds, p, 3ds, join to 4th p of previous r, 3ds, p, 3ds, join to 2nd p of 1st r, 3ds, p, 3ds, cl. RW.

5th chain: as 1st ch, join to 1st ch at base of 1st r. Without breaking the thread continue into the 1st round.

1st round

* *Chain:* 3ds, p, 5ds, p, 5ds; then, using the 2nd shuttle:

Small ring: 3ds, 4p sep by 3ds, 3ds, cl.

Continue the chain with the 1st shuttle, 5ds, p, 5ds, p, 3ds, join to the next sp between the ch on the centre motif.

Rep from * 4 times. Tie ends and cut short.

2nd round

Using shuttle thread of the same colour as the centre group of rings, and a ball thread of the second colour, start with the ring arrowed on Illustration 78.

1st ring: 7ds, join to the left-hand p of a small ring on the 1st round, 7ds, cl. RW.

** *1st chain*: 2ds, 5p sep by 2ds, 2ds. RW.

* *Ring:* 7ds, join to next p of same small ring, 7ds, cl. RW.

Chain: as 1st ch.

Rep from * twice, then without reversing join to the p between the two sets of 5ds on the ch of the 1st round.

Chain: 8ds, join to the p between the two sets of 5ds on the next ch of the 1st round.

Chain: 2ds, 2p sep by 2ds, 2ds, join to the 3rd p of the adjacent ch of the 2nd round, 2ds, 2p sep by 2ds, 2ds. RW.

Ring: 7ds, join to left-hand p of the next small r of the 1st round, 7ds, cl. RW.

Rep from ** 4 times, omitting the last r on the final rep, and completing the round by joining the last ch to the 1st ch at the base of the 1st r. Tie ends and cut short. Glue all the ends neatly to one side. Damp the work, pull into shape and leave to dry.

To complete the box

Place the motif on the backing material and fix inside the lid as detailed in the instructions with the box.

5 Jewellery

BROOCH

The same pattern is used for the brooch as was described for the trinket box decoration. The brooch was worked all in white, and after the whole motif had been completed the centre was mounted onto a piece of card covered in black felt.

Materials

No. 60 crochet thread in white or selected colour
Piece of stiff card, approximately 1in (2.5cm) square
Piece of felt in black or selected colour, approximately 2in (5cm) square
Small safety pin, $\frac{3}{4}$in (18mm) long

To make the brooch

Using only one colour of thread, start by half filling the two shuttles with an unbroken thread. Work as instructed for the trinket box decoration, but ignore all the references to working with two colours.

79 A motif mounted and worn as a brooch

To complete the brooch

Cut a circle of card with $\frac{4}{5}$in (20mm) diameter and a circle of felt with $1\frac{3}{10}$in (3.2cm) diameter. Cover the card with the felt as detailed in the round picture frame pattern on page 61. Place the motif centrally onto the covered card and, using thread the same colour as the felt, attach the motif to the felt by the centre picots on the chains of the centre motif and by the two free picots on the chains of the 1st round. Cut a circle of felt the same size as the card and sew it to the back of the brooch. Sew the safety pin to the centre of the back, making sure that it does not show at the front. After first checking that the felt is colour fast, spray starch the brooch and leave to dry.

80 Star earrings and fob

STAR EARRINGS AND FOB

The earrings are made from a motif which is composed of a tatted ring with beads and picots alternating; chains are then joined into these picots around the ring. The same motif forms the centre of the fob, which is then joined by the picots on the chains to a curtain ring whilst the ring is being covered with double crochet or buttonhole stitch. The tatted edging of the fob is decorated with picots and beads and is worked directly onto the covered ring.

Materials

No. 40 crochet thread in black or selected colour
32 gold beads, size P$2\frac{1}{2}$
Brass curtain ring, $\frac{7}{8}$in (2.2cm) internal diameter
Gilt bow with jump ring
Pair of gilt earrings with hanging facility
No. 1.00mm crochet hook or sewing needle

Measurements

Earring motif – $\frac{3}{4}$in (18mm) diameter
Fob motif – $1\frac{1}{2}$in (3.7cm) diameter

Earring motif

Two of these are made – see Illustration 81. Thread six beads onto the working thread, wind a small amount of thread onto the shuttle and do not cut off from the ball.
Ring: put the six beads on the ring thread, 1ds, slide a bead around the r, 1ds, * sm p, 1ds, bead, 1ds, rep from * 4 times (6 beads and 5 sm p on r), cl. RW.
Chain: sm p, 5ds, p, 5ds, * join to next p on r, 5ds, p, 5ds, rep from* 3 times, join to next p on r (thus 5 chains are made around r).
6th chain: 5ds, p long enough when closed to hold one bead + $\frac{1}{8}$in (3mm), 5ds, join to sm p made at the beg of the 1st ch.

Tie ends, cut short and glue neatly to the back.

81 Diagram showing construction details of the star earrings and fob

Fob

Work a motif as for the earring, but make all six chains the same. Join this motif evenly, by the picots on the chains, to the curtain ring, while at the same time covering the ring with neat double crochet or buttonhole stitch as detailed in the pattern for the Christmas decoration on page 35. Fasten off and secure the ends neatly to the back.

Fob edging

Thread 12 beads onto the working thread, wind a small amount of thread onto the shuttle and do not cut off from the ball. To help keep the chain loops evenly spaced around the ring, relate all joins to the centre motif.

* Join to the covered ring at a point where the centre motif is joined to the ring, then slide a bead along.
Chain: 3ds, 3 graduated p sep by 1ds, 3ds, join to the ring between the points of the centre motif, then slide another bead along.
Chain: 3ds, 3 graduated p sep by 1ds, 3ds.

Rep from * around the ring until one ch remains to be made.
Last chain: join to the ring, 8ds, then join to the same place as the 1st join was made.

Tie the ends, cut short and glue neatly to the back. Damp and shape the work, pulling out all chains and picots evenly. Stiffen and leave to dry.

To complete

Earrings

Put a bead onto the long picot of the 6th chain, strengthen the remaining section of picot with clear glue, then hang the motif by this picot onto the earring. Close up the hanging loop of the earring.

Fob

Place the jump ring on the last chain of the fob motif, attach the bow to the ring and close up the ring securely.

PENDANT AND EARRINGS

The pendant motif and the earrings are made from the same pattern. The centre of the motif is made of one tatted ring with long picots, which are for decoration but are also used for joining the tatted ring to a curtain ring whilst this is being covered with double crochet or buttonhole stitch. The picots, therefore, must be of a size to fill the curtain ring but still lie neatly within it (see Illustration 83). The tatted edging of the motif is worked directly onto the covered ring. The beads are added after the tatting has been worked.

Materials

No. 20 crochet thread in black or selected colour
Seven silver beads, size P3
Three brass curtain rings, $\frac{5}{8}$in (15mm) external diameter
Pair of silver earrings with hanging facility
Necklace chain with jump ring
No. 1.00mm crochet hook or sewing needle

Measurements

Motif – $1\frac{1}{4}$in (3cm) diameter

82 Matching pendant and earrings

Centre

Wind a small amount of thread onto the shuttle and leave about 4in (10cm) at the start.

Ring: 1ds, 6 l p sep by 2ds, 1ds, cl.

Cut the working thread to about 4in (10cm) long, put a bead onto this thread and lay it across the ring so that the bead lies across the centre, then take this thread through the picot opposite and to the back of the work. Tie the two ends of thread together in a firm knot close to the work; glue the knot and cut the ends very short.

Join the centre to the curtain ring evenly by the picots, at the same time as covering the ring with double crochet or buttonhole stitch as detailed in the pattern for the Christmas decoration on page 35. Fasten off and secure the ends neatly to the back.

Edging

Join the chains of the edging as shown in Illustration 83. Wind a small amount of thread onto the shuttle and do not cut off from the ball. Join to the covered ring and work:

Chains 1, 3, 5, 7: 7ds.

Chains 2, 4, 6: 2ds, 5p sep by 1ds, 2ds.

Chain 8: (a) for the earrings – 4ds, p long enough when closed to hold one bead + ⅛in (3mm);

(b) for the pendant – 4ds, p long enough when closed to hold 2 beads + ⅛in (3mm).

N.B. The size of this chain may be adjusted to fit the remaining space on the ring.

Tie ends, cut short and glue neatly to the back. Damp and shape the motifs, pulling out all chains and picots evenly.

To complete

Earrings

Put one bead onto the long p of the 8th chain, strengthen the remaining section of picot with clear glue, then hang the motif by this picot to the earring. Close up the hanging loop of the earring.

Necklace pendant

Put two beads onto the long p of the 8th chain, strengthen the remaining section of picot with clear glue and put the jump ring through it. Thread the necklace through the jump ring and close up the ring securely.

83 Diagram showing construction details of the pendant

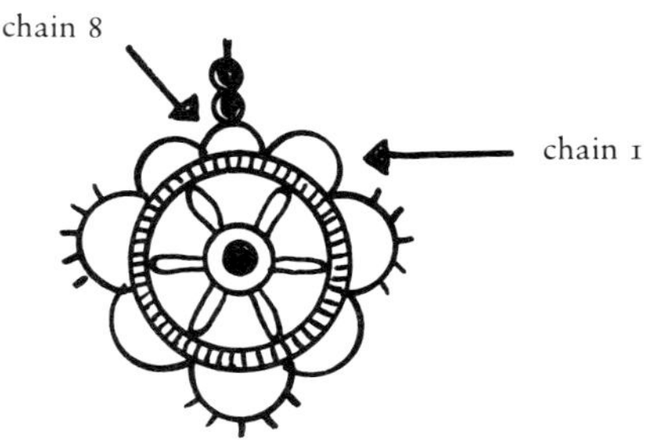

84 Brooch with a centre of pearls

PEARL CENTRE BROOCH

The brooch has a central tatted ring with beads and picots alternating. The beads are the main feature of the centre and should fit snugly inside the covered curtain ring. The petals are constructed from three rounds of chains with picots; regular size picots enhance the look of the petals.

Materials

No. 40 crochet thread in selected colour
Seven pearl beads, size P3½
Brass curtain ring, ⅝in (15mm) external diameter
No. 1.00mm crochet hook or sewing needle
Small safety pin

Measurement

2in (5cm) diameter

The brooch centre

Thread six beads onto the working thread, put a small amount of thread onto the shuttle and do not cut off from the ball.

Ring: put the six beads onto the ring thread, * 1ds, bead, 1ds, 1 p, (p to be longer, when closed, than the height of the bead), rep from * until the six beads have been used and five picots made. Close the r and form the 6th p by tying the two threads together. Leaving 10in (25cm) thread, cut the shuttle thread, put the 7th bead onto this thread and position it over the centre of the ring, then take the thread through the picot opposite to hold the bead in place. Leave the end for sewing the pin to the back of the brooch.

Using the ball thread, join the centre to the curtain ring at the same time as covering the ring with double crochet; or cut the ball thread and cover with buttonhole stitch as detailed in the pattern for the Christmas decoration on page 35.

Petal edging

Relate the position of the petals to the beads of the centre to ensure an even distribution. Using ball and shuttle thread, start by joining to the covered ring slightly to the left of a bead on the centre (see Illustration 85).

1st round of petals

* *Petal chain:* 2ds, 7p sep by 2ds, 2ds, join to

85 Diagram showing construction details of the pearl centre brooch

the ring to the right of the bead.
Chain between petals: 2ds, sm p, 1ds, join to the ring over the next p of the centre, 1ds, sm p, 2ds, join to the ring over the left-hand side of the next bead.

Rep from * until six petals and chains between have been completed. Join the last chain to the base of the 1st petal and then draw the ball thread back through the last picot made, ready to work:

2nd round of petals

* *Petal chain:* 2ds, 11p sep by 2ds, 2ds, join to the next p of the ch between the petals of the 1st round.
Chain between petals: 1ds, sm p, 1ds, join to next p of next ch of 1st round.

Rep from * until six petals and chains between have been completed. Join the last chain to the base of the 1st petal of this round and then draw the ball thread back through the last picot made, ready to work:

3rd round of petals

* *Petal chain:* 2ds, 16p sep by 2ds, 2ds, join to the p of the ch between the petals of the 2nd round.

Rep from * until six petals have been completed. Join the last petal to the base of the 1st petal of this round.

To complete

Glue all ends neatly to the back. Sew a small pin to the centre back. Starch and shape the petals.

BEADED CHOKER AND HAIR DECORATION

The choker and the hair decoration are made from the same pattern, which can also be used as a beaded braid on fashion accessories if preferred. The larger beads in the centre of the braid are added to long picots on the centre rings after each ring has been completed. The clusters of three small beads on the chains are added whilst the chains are being constructed, and so the small beads must be put onto the ball thread before work commences. The double stitches on the rings are made in the usual way, but on the chains there are groups or sets of half stitches, i.e. three first-half stitches are made and then three second-half stitches, followed by a further three first-half stitches. This is written in the pattern as 3.3.3. Working stitches in this way gives a zigzag effect to one side of the chain and keeps the chain straighter.

Materials

No. 20 crochet thread in selected colour
220 small beads, size P2 } for the
33 larger beads, size P3 } choker
80 small beads, size P2 } for the hair
9 larger beads, size P3 } decoration
3in (7.5cm) comb or slide
Piece of felt to back the braid for the comb or slide

Measurements

Choker – $12\frac{1}{2}$in × 1in (31.2cm × 2.5cm)
Hair decoration – $3\frac{1}{2}$in × 1in (8.6cm × 2.5cm)

The choker

The centre rings and one side of the braid are constructed first; the second side is then worked without breaking the thread. Put 200 small beads onto the working thread and fill the shuttle. The long picots on the rings must be long enough to hold a larger bead and allow a join to be made.

1st side

1st ring: 3ds, l p, 3ds, sm p, 3ds, l p, 3ds, cl. RW.

* *Chain:* sets of half stitches, 3.3.3., slide 3 beads into place, 3.3.3. RW.

Next ring: 3ds, put a bead onto the last p of the previous r then join to this p, 3ds, sm p, 3ds, l p, 3ds, cl. RW.

Rep from * until 32 rings have been made.

1st end

(Illustration 87B)

Next chain: as previous chains, then put a bead onto the l p of the last r and join to it. Make one more ch as before and join to the sm p of the last r.

2nd side

* *Chain:* 3.3.3., 3 bead cluster, 3.3.3., join to sm p of next r.

86 Beaded choker

A

B

87 Diagram showing construction details of the hair decoration (A) and the choker (B)

Rep from * all along the side until all the rings have been joined.

2nd end
Complete as for 1st end but finish by joining the 1st ch at the base of the 1st r. Tie ends and cut.

Ties
Work one of these for each end.
Put nine small beads onto the working thread and wind a small amount of thread onto the shuttle.

End motif
Ring: 4ds, 2 sm p sep by 4ds, 4ds, cl. RW. * *Chain:* 3.3.3., 3 bead cluster, 3.3.3., join to 1st sm p of r, rep from * once, joining to 2nd sm p and again joining to 1st ch at base of r. Continue to make a length of chain (8in or 20cm long) for the ties by working sets of 3.3. Join to the choker between the two end chains. Tie ends and cut short.

To complete the choker
Glue the ends to one side. Damp the work and shape the chains evenly with the clusters coming off the chains neatly.

Hair decoration
Put 60 small beads onto the working thread and half fill the shuttle. Work as for the choker until eight rings have been made. Work the end in the same way but add a cluster of three beads between the two end chains (see Illustration 87A). Complete the second side as for the choker, and then the second end remembering the cluster of beads between the two end chains.

Dangle
Put 18 beads onto the working thread and wind a small amount of thread onto the shuttle. Working from the instructions for the choker ties, make an end motif and 2in (5cm) chain, join to the braid at the base of an end ring (see Illustration 87A), then work a further $1\frac{1}{2}$in (3.7cm) chain and another end motif. Tie ends and cut short.

To complete the hair decoration
Glue the ends to the back. Damp the work and shape the chains evenly with the clusters coming off the chains neatly. Cover the comb or slide with a piece of felt and glue the braid centrally to it.

88 Beaded hair decoration

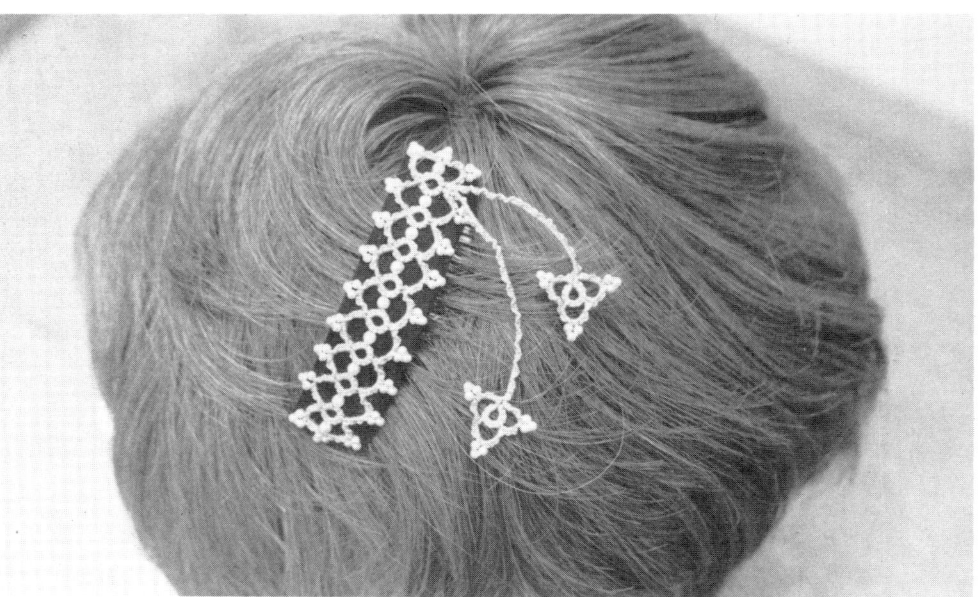

6 Pictures

A BOUQUET OF SPRING FLOWERS

These three-dimensional flowers are tatted interpretations of daffodils, narcissi and hyacinths. The daffodils have large trumpet centres and the narcissi have smaller trumpet or flat centres. The flowers are made in colours as near to nature as possible. The originals were mounted onto a piece of dark brown Fablon Velour and framed to make a picture (see Illustration 89). Different combinations of flowers can be used to make a more individual picture or to decorate an Easter cake or card.

Materials

Daffodil – No. 40 crochet thread in yellow and green
Narcissus – No. 40 crochet thread in gold, white and green
Hyacinth – No. 20 crochet thread in blue and green
Picture frame, $7\frac{1}{2}$in × 6in (18.7cm × 15cm)
Piece of covered card to fit inside the frame
Fablon Velour oval, $5\frac{1}{2}$ × 4in (13.7cm × 10cm)
12in (30cm) narrow ribbon, old gold colour
No. 1.00mm crochet hook or sewing needle

Measurements

Daffodil flower – $1\frac{1}{4}$in × $1\frac{1}{4}$in × $\frac{5}{8}$in (3cm × 3cm × 15mm)
Narcissus flower – 1in × 1in × $\frac{3}{8}$in (2.5cm × 2.5cm × 9mm)
Hyacinth stem of flowers – $1\frac{1}{4}$in × $\frac{3}{8}$in (3cm × 9mm)

Daffodil

(make two)
The trumpet centre is made first and the petals made around it without breaking the thread. Wind a small amount of yellow thread onto the shuttle and do not cut off from the ball.

89 A Bouquet of Spring Flowers

Trumpet centre
(Illustration 90)
Ring: 2ds, 11p sep by 2ds, 2ds, cl. Form a 12th p by tying the two working threads together in a tight knot.
1st chain: 3ds, p, 3ds, 5p sep by 1ds, 3ds, p, 3ds, join to 12th p of r, * 2ds, miss 1p on r, join to next p.
Next chain: (3ds, join to adjacent p of previous ch) twice, 1ds, 4p sep by 1ds, 3ds, p, 3ds, join to same p as start of this ch.

Rep from * 4 times *but on the final rep* (6th ch) replace the last 2p by joining to the 1st 2p of the 1st ch.

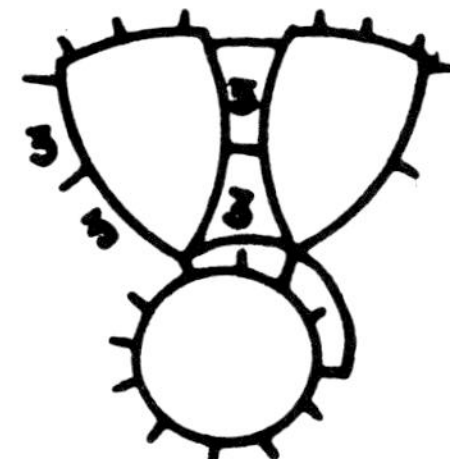

90 Diagram showing the construction of the daffodil trumpet around the centre ring

91 Diagram showing the position of the petals around the trumpet centre of both the daffodil and narcissus. The dotted lines indicate the section of petal underneath

Petals
(Illustration 91)
Working around the outside of the trumpet centre, make 2ds and join to the next free p on r.
* *Chain:* 11ds, sm p, 11ds, *miss next free p on r*, and join to following free p, rep from * twice but join 3rd petal to p where 1st petal started. Then working over the 3 petals just made, make 3ds, join to next free p on r.
** *Chain:* 11ds, sm p, 11ds, join to next free p on r, rep from ** twice but join the last petal to p where 4th petal started. Tie ends and cut.

Stem
Using green thread join into the last p used on the r. Work either double crochet or buttonhole stitch over the ends of the thread from the flower for $2\frac{1}{2}$in (6.2cm). Fasten off and glue or sew ends neatly to the back.

Narcissus with trumpet centre
(make two)
The trumpet centre is made first out of gold thread, then the gold ball thread is substituted with white thread for making the petals.

92 Diagram showing the construction of the narcissus trumpet around the centre ring

Trumpet centre
(Illustration 92)
Wind a small amount of gold thread onto the shuttle and do not cut off from the ball.
Ring: 1ds, 11p sep by 1ds, 1ds, cl. Form a 12th p by tying the two working threads together in a tight knot.
1st chain: 3ds, 3p sep by 1ds, 3ds, * miss 1p on r, join to next p.
Next chain: 3ds, join to adjacent p of previous ch, 1ds, 2p sep by 1ds, 3ds.

Rep from * 4 times but on the final rep (6th ch) replace the last p by joining to the 1st p of the 1st ch, and join the last ch to the 12th p of the r.

** Cut off the ball thread and replace it with white thread.

Petals
Working around the outside of the centre join to the next free p on r.
* *Chain:* 9ds, sm p, 9ds, miss next free p on r, join to following free p, rep from * twice but join 3rd petal to p where 1st petal started. Then working over the 3 petals just made, work 3ds and join to next free p on r.
* *Chain:* 9ds, sm p, 9ds, join to next free p on r, rep from * twice but join the last ch to p where 4th petal started. Tie ends and cut.

Stem
Work as daffodil stem.

Narcissus with flat centre

(make one)
Prepare the threads and work the ring as for the narcissus with trumpet centre.
* *Chain:* 5ds, miss 1p on r, join to next p, rep from * 5 times, join last ch to 12th p of r. Continue by working from ** in the pattern for the narcissus with trumpet centre, making the petals under and around the flat centre.

Hyacinth

(make two)
Wind sufficient blue thread onto the shuttle to make 11 small rings, tie the end to the ball of green thread and start with the top ring (see Illustration 93).

93 Diagram showing the construction of the hyacinth

Top:
* *Ring:* (blue) 3ds, p, 3ds, cl. RW.
Chain: (green) 2ds. RW.
1st side:
Rep from * twice, then work a further three slightly larger rings of 4ds, p, 4ds, with a ch of 2ds between each of them.
Stem chain: 4ds, p, 4ds, p, 8ds, twist ch around and join to the last p made on the stem, 4ds, join to next p on stem, 4ds, join to the gap in the stem opposite the last r made. RW.
2nd side:
* *Ring:* 4ds, p, 4ds, cl. RW.
Chain: 2ds, join to gap in stem opposite next r on 1st side. RW.
Rep from * twice, then work a further two rings of 3ds, p, 3ds, with one ch of 2ds between them. Join to 1st side opposite 2nd r made. Tie ends, cut short and glue securely to one side.

To complete the picture

Spray each piece of tatting with starch. Shape the petals and the trumpets of the daffodils and narcissi. Arrange the flowers of the hyacinths so that they lie at different angles to the stem. When the flowers are dry arrange them on the oval piece of Fablon and carefully glue them in place. Tie a bow with the piece of ribbon and glue it across the stems. Fix the Fablon to the centre of the covered card. Remove the glass from the picture frame, insert the picture and secure.

A SUMMER CORNER

The butterfly and the flowers in the picture (Illustration 94) are worked in No. 40 crochet threads in gold, cream and ecru. The butterfly alone looks effective when applied to the pocket of a skirt, or to underwear when worked in a finer thread.

Materials

Butterfly – No. 40 crochet thread in gold
Flowers – small amounts of No. 40 crochet thread in gold, cream and ecru

94 A Summer Corner

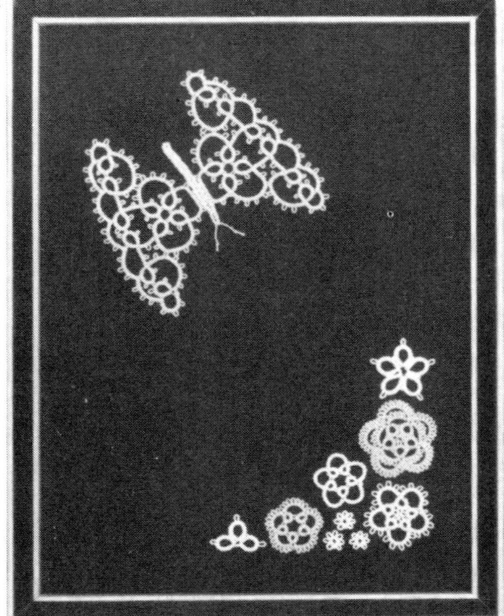

Picture frame, $8\frac{1}{2}$in × $6\frac{1}{2}$in (21.2cm × 16.2cm)
Piece of stiff card slightly smaller than the frame
Piece of dark material or felt to cover the card

Measurements

Butterfly – $2\frac{3}{4}$in × 3in (6.8cm × 7.5cm)
Flowers – from approximately $\frac{1}{4}$in to $1\frac{1}{4}$in (6mm to 3cm)

Butterfly

Worked in gold thread, the two wings are made separately and joined to the body after being completed.

Wings
(make two the same)
Work from the following notes in conjunction with the diagram of the wing at Illustration 95, starting at the ring marked 1.

1. Reverse the work after each ring and chain.
2. *The picots* are all the same length although those used for joining are shown longer on the diagram.
3. *The rings* are all constructed in the same way – 4ds, p, 4ds, p, 2ds, p, 4ds, p, 4ds – but note from the diagram where they join each other.
4. *The chains:* except for chain 5, chains 1–9 are either 'long' or 'short'. Each long chain (e.g. chain 1) is 3ds, 6p sep by 3ds, 3ds, and each short chain (e.g. chain 2) is 3ds, p, 3ds. Note from the diagram where they join each other.

Chain 5: 3ds, p, 3ds, 4p sep by 2ds, 3ds, p, 3ds.
Chains 10–16: 3ds, 3p sep by 3ds, 3ds, join to rings 10, 9, 8, 3, 2 and 1 as shown in the diagram.

Body
The body is made from one ring. The wings are joined by five of the picots of the 5th chain during the construction of the body ring, as follows:
Ring: leave 2in (5cm) thread at the start – this will form one antenna. 6ds, join to the 2nd p

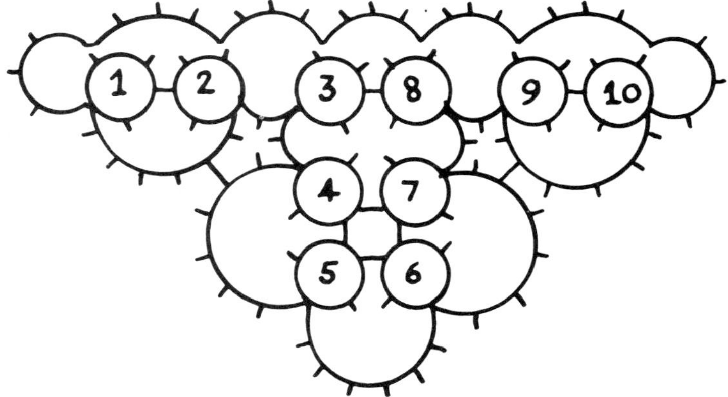

95 Diagram showing construction details of the butterfly wing

of the 5th ch of one wing, * 2ds, join to next p on wing, rep from * twice, 3ds, join to last p on wing, 36ds, join to 1st p on 5th ch of second wing, 3ds, ** join to next p, 2ds, rep from ** twice, join to next p, 6ds, close the ring carefully. Cut the thread leaving an end of 2in (5cm) for the second antenna.

To complete the butterfly

The first 4ds and the last 4ds of the body ring form the head of the butterfly. Carefully glue or sew together all the remaining ds of the ring, making sure that the wings lie evenly on either side. To form the antennae tie an overhand knot ¼in (6mm) from the head and then trim the threads so that the total length of each antenna is ⅜in (9mm). Cut all other ends short and glue neatly to one side. Damp the work, shape the chains evenly and pull out the picots.

The flowers

These are all variations of simple motifs. Instructions are given for those shown (see Illustration 96), but any variety can be used to make a more individual picture.

Flower 1

(make one in cream)

Ring: 4ds, 3p sep by 5ds, 4ds, cl.

* *Ring:* 4ds, join to last p of previous r, 5ds, 2p sep by 5ds, 4ds, cl.

Rep from * 3 times joining last r to 1st r. Tie ends and cut short.

Flower 2

(make one in cream)

1st ring: 8ds, p, 5ds, p, 3ds, cl.

2nd ring: 3ds, join to last p of 1st r, 5ds, p, 5ds, p, 3ds, cl.

3rd ring: 3ds, join to last p of 2nd r, 5ds, p, 8ds, cl. Tie ends and cut short.

Flower 3

(make three in cream)

Ring: 1ds, 7p sep by 1ds, 1ds, cl. Tie ends and cut short.

Flower 4

(make one in gold)

1st ring: 3ds, 2p sep by 3ds, 3ds, cl. RW.

1st chain: 1ds, 7p sep by 1ds, 1ds. RW.

* *Next ring:* 3ds, join to last p of previous r, 3ds, p, 3ds, cl. RW.

Next chain: as 1st ch.

Rep from * 3 times, joining last r to 1st r and last ch to 1st ch at base of 1st r. Tie ends and cut short.

Flower 5

(make one in gold)

1st ring: 3ds, 3p sep by 3ds, 3ds, cl. RW.

1st chain: 1ds, 5p sep by 1ds, 1ds. RW.

* *Next ring:* 3ds, join to last p of previous r, 3ds, 2p sep by 3ds, 3ds, cl. RW.

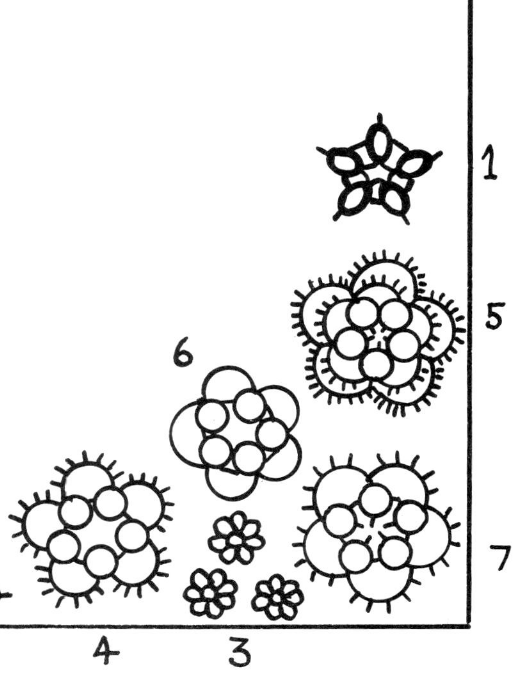

96 The arrangement of the flower motifs in the Summer Corner picture

97 Misty Morn

Next chain: as 1st ch.

Rep from * 3 times joining last r to 1st r and last ch to 1st ch at base of 1st r.

Second round: over each existing ch work another *chain:* 1ds, 11p sep by 1ds, 1ds, join to sp between ch of 1st round. Tie ends and cut short.

Flower 6

(make one in ecru)

1st ring: 3ds, 2p sep by 3ds, 3ds, cl. RW.

1st chain: 10ds. RW.

* *Next ring:* 3ds, join to last p of previous r, 3ds, p, 3ds, cl. RW.

Next chain: as 1st ch.

Rep from * 3 times, joining last r to 1st r and last ch to 1st ch at base of 1st r. Tie ends and cut short.

Flower 7

(make one in ecru)

1st ring: 3ds, 3p sep by 2ds, 3ds, cl. RW.

1st chain: 2ds, 5p sep by 2ds, 2ds. RW.

* *Next ring:* 3ds, join to last p of previous r, 2ds, 2p sep by 2ds, 3ds, cl. RW.

Next chain: as 1st ch.

Rep from * 3 times, joining last r to 1st r and last ch to 1st ch at base of 1st r. Tie ends and cut short.

To complete the flowers

Glue all ends neatly to one side. Damp and shape each piece.

To complete the picture

Cut the piece of stiff card to fit inside the frame. Glue the covering material to the card and trim. Arrange the tatting as desired on the covered card and carefully glue in position.

MISTY MORN

This is a tatted interpretation of a misty autumn morning when everything seems white and grey, and the sun is just hinting that it will clear the mist in an hour or so. The tatting was worked in white threads, with beads indicating the sun's presence, and was mounted onto a piece of card covered in grey silk which was framed in a white card.

Materials

Twilley's Lyscordet in white (for the grass)
No. 40 crochet thread in white
White pearl beads, 23 size P2, two size P3, one size P01
Piece of card, $8\frac{1}{2}$in × $4\frac{1}{4}$in (21.2cm × 10.6cm)

covered in grey material
CRAFTacard, size $7\frac{3}{4}$in × 6in (19.3cm × 15cm)

The grass

This is simply a length of chain with picots of various sizes (to give different lengths of grasses) separated by one or two double stitches. The picots are cut open and should range from $\frac{1}{4}$in–$\frac{3}{4}$in (6mm–18mm) after being cut. Make the chain out of the Lyscordet, long enough to fit across the bottom of the backing card. Cut the picots open.

The moth

Thread two large and two small beads onto the working thread in the following order; one large, two small, one large. Wind a small amount of thread onto the shuttle and do not cut off from the ball.

Ring: put the beads onto the ring thread, 2ds, l p (to be cut open later for the antennae), 3ds, sm p, 1ds, large bead, 1ds, sm p, 1ds, small bead, 1ds, sm p, 1ds, small bead, 1ds, sm p, 1ds, large bead, 1ds, cl. RW.

Set of chains: these are worked around the r joining to the sm p in turn, 22ds, join, 18ds, join, 18ds, join, 22ds, join.

Tie the ends, cut short and glue to the back. Cut the long picot of the ring for the antennae.

Large flower

(make one)

Put five small beads onto the working thread, wind a small amount of thread onto the shuttle and do not cut off from the ball.

Ring: put the beads onto the ring thread, * 1ds, bead, 1ds, sm p, rep from * until the last bead has been used, 1ds (5 beads and 4 sm p), cl. RW.

1st round of chains: these are worked round the r, sm p, * 10ds, join to next sm p on r, rep from * all round the r, joining the last ch to the sm p made at the beginning of the round. Continue into:

2nd round of chains: sm p, * 14ds, join to sp between ch of 1st round, rep from * joining last ch to sm p. Continue the ch to form a stem of $2\frac{3}{4}$in (6.8cm). Tie ends and cut short.

Small flower

(make one)

Wind a small amount of thread onto the shuttle and do not cut off from the ball.

98 Diagram showing the construction details of the tatting in the Misty Morn picture

Ring: 1ds, * p, 1ds, rep from * 3 times, cl. RW.
Chains: these are worked round the r, sm p, * 6ds, join to p on r, rep from * all round r, join last ch to sm p made at start. Continue the ch to form a stem of 2in (5cm).

Tie ends and cut short. Glue a small bead to the centre of the ring.

Tiny flower

(make eight)
The tiny flowers are rings with a length of thread for the stem.
Ring: leave 2in (5cm) thread, 1ds, 6p sep by 2ds, 1ds, cl. Cut leaving 3in (7.5cm) thread for the stem. Put a small bead on the 2in (5cm) length of thread, allow the bead to lie on the centre of the ring, put the end of thread through the picot opposite and tie the two ends together to keep the bead in place. Cut the short end to ¼in (6mm) and glue to the back.

Leaves

(make two)
The leaves are constructed alike except that one has a bead at the tip which must be put onto the working thread before starting the outer edge.
Centre: put three small beads onto the working thread, wind sufficient thread onto the shuttle to make three rings and put the three beads at intervals along it.
* *Ring:* 3ds, 3p sep by 3ds, 3ds, cl. Slide a bead along to lie in the centre of the r, turn work over and join to 2nd p to hold the bead in place; turn work back again, rep from * twice. Cut the thread.
Outer edging: use ball and shuttle thread, with a bead on the ball thread for the tip of the leaf, if required. Start at the base of the leaf and work along the left-hand side of the centre.
Chain: sm p (use a sm p spacer, e.g. a cocktail stick, and leave it in place until the join into the sm p is made), 5ds, join to p of 1st r, 7ds, join to p of 2nd r, 7ds, join to p of 3rd r, 4ds, join to end of 3rd r, place bead (if required). Now work down the right-hand side joining to each r in turn, 4ds, join, 7ds, join, 6ds, join, 4ds, join to sm p made at the start. Continue the ch to form a stem of 1½in (3.7cm). Tie ends and cut short.

Tiny creature

Use only shuttle thread, leave 1½in (3.7cm) thread for the tail before starting the ring.
Ring: 6ds, 2p (for ears) sep by 1ds, 3ds, p (for nose), 11ds, close r carefully ensuring that the oval bead will fit snugly inside it to form the body. Cut the thread to 3in (7.5cm) and put the oval bead onto it, take the thread through the nose picot and then cut this thread short and glue it to the back.

To complete the card

Damp all the pieces of tatting, pull out the picots and shape the chains evenly, particularly on the moth. Arrange the flowers, leaves and moth on the piece of covered card. Carefully glue each piece in place. Glue the grass across the bottom, covering all the ends of the stems. Glue the tiny creature in the grass, weave its tail in and out of the grass and secure the end in place with glue.

CHRISTMAS DECORATION OF POINSETTIAS AND MISTLETOE

The poinsettias and mistletoe were designed to be used on a Christmas cake but they could also be used on Christmas cards or on serviette rings to decorate a Christmas table. The decoration shown in Illustration 99 was used on a 6in (15cm) diameter cake covered in green icing. Since the decoration is arranged and glued onto a piece of covered card it was easy to remove when the cake was cut and thereafter was used as a table decoration. The cake frill is made out of cream ribbon to contrast with the icing on the cake whilst at the same time providing a good background for the green and red tatting.

99 Christmas decoration of poinsettias and mistletoe

100 Diagram showing the construction of the poinsettia flower

101 Diagram showing the construction of the poinsettia centre

Materials

No. 40 crochet thread in red, dark green and gold for the poinsettias and light green for the mistletoe
15 white pearl beads, size P2
4in (10cm) red candle
Plasticine
6in × 1in (15cm × 2.5cm) taffeta ribbon in cream
Piece of stiff card 4in (10cm) diameter covered in cream material

Measurements

Poinsettia with leaves – approximately $1\frac{1}{2}$in (3.7cm)
Mistletoe – $\frac{1}{2}$in × $1\frac{1}{2}$in (1.2cm × 3.7cm)

Poinsettia flower

(make two large and one small – Illustration 100)
The instructions for the smaller flower are given in brackets. Work in red thread.
Ring: 2ds, 9p sep by 2ds, 2ds, cl. RW.
Chain: sm p, * 10(8)ds, p, 10(8)ds, miss 1p on the r, join to next p, rep from * 4 times, join the last ch to the sm p made at the start (5 petals). Fold the 1st petal forward and at the back carefully take both threads across to the next free p on the r and join. The next round of chains is worked behind the previous round.
Chain: * 13(10)ds, p, 13(10)ds, join to next free p on r. Rep from * 4 times, join the last ch to the p on the r used at the beg of the round. Tie ends and cut.

Poinsettia centre

(make three – Illustration 101)
Work with gold thread.
Ring: leave 1in (2.5cm) thread at the start. 1ds, 6p each $1\frac{1}{2}$in (3.7cm) long sep by 1ds, 1ds, cl. Leave 1in (2.5cm) thread and cut.

Cut each picot at its centre. Tie an overhand knot on each piece of picot and at the two ends. Trim ends close to the knots.

102 Diagram showing the construction of the poinsettia leaves

103 Diagram showing the construction of the mistletoe and the final shaping

Poinsettia leaves

(make three – Illustration 102)
Work with dark green thread.
Ring: 4ds, 4p sep by 4ds, 4ds, cl. RW.
Chain: sm p, * 16ds, p, 16ds, join to next p on r, rep from * 4 times, join the 5th ch to the sm p made at the start. Tie ends and cut.

To complete the flowers

Cut the ends on the flowers and leaves very short and glue neatly to the back. Damp the work and shape all the chains into points, pulling out the picots to accentuate the shape. Arrange the petals of the flowers so that the top five stand proud of the lower five. Leave to dry. Glue the gold centre to the middle of the flower and then glue the flower to the centre of the leaves.

Mistletoe sprigs

(make 11, varying the lengths of the stems – Illustration 103)
Work with light green thread.

Following the diagram, start at the arrow and make a chain of about 1½in (3.7cm) for the stem, then a ring of 2ds, 3p sep by 1ds, 2ds, cl. Make a chain of 18ds and join to the base of the ring so that the chain lies as a loop to the left of the ring, then make a further chain of 18ds and join to the base of the ring so that it lies as a loop to the right of the ring. Tie ends and cut short.

To complete the mistletoe

Glue the ends to the back. Damp each piece and arrange the chain loops to the right and left of the ring so that they curve round the ring as shown in the diagram.

To make up the decoration

Cover the card as detailed in the pattern for the round picture frame. Roll the plastercine into a ball of sufficient size to support the candle. Push the candle into the plastercine ball then flatten the base so that it stands firmly. Make the cover for the plastercine as follows: sew the two ends of the ribbon together with running stitches to form a circle, then turn the seam to the inside; run a separate gathering thread along each edge, place the plastercine inside the ribbon ring, and pull up the gathering threads so that the plastercine is completely covered. Fasten off the ends securely. Arrange the tatting on the piece of covered card, placing all the ends of the mistletoe so that they will be covered by the candle holder. Glue the tatting in place with the candle holder on top. Glue clusters of three pearls at intervals along the mistletoe stems.

Cake frill

The cake frill is made out of strips of tafetta ribbon and the tatting is applied to the centre strip. Any pattern for a tatted insertion can be used but the width of the centre strip of ribbon on the frill must be slightly wider than the tatting. The tatting used on the cake frill shown in Illustration 99 was worked from a traditional pattern but using two colours, red and green, and was adapted to include beads so that it matched the decoration on top of the cake.

Materials

1in × 4yd (2.5cm × 3.7m), or six times the length of finished frill size, tafetta ribbon

Measurements

2½in × 22½in (6.2cm × 55.2cm), if length has not been adjusted.

To make the frill

1. Cut one piece of ribbon 24in (60cm) long, or the length of frill required plus a small hem allowance. Cut two pieces twice the length of the first piece.
2. Run a gathering thread ¼in (6mm) in from one edge on each of the two long pieces. Draw up the gathering thread evenly so that the gathered ribbon fits along the short piece of ribbon.
3. Turn these three pieces of ribbon to the wrong side. Lay a gathered piece along each side of, and slightly on top of, the straight piece. Pin into position and sew in place.
4. Take another piece of ribbon, the same length as the first shorter piece, and attach the tatting to the right side of it. Glue or sew this piece of ribbon to the right side of the frill.
5. Turn over a small hem to the back of each end of the completed frill.

To protect the frill, fasten a piece of greaseproof paper round the cake before adding the frill.

Suppliers

Dryad
P.O. Box 38
Northgates
Leicester LE1 9BU
England

Dryad offer a comprehensive range of craft requirements by post.

D.J. Hornsby
149 High Street
Burton Latimer
Kettering
Northants NN15 5RL
England

D.J. Hornsby, Sebalace and A. Sells are specialist lace suppliers who will supply general tatting requirements by post. Send a large stamped, addressed envelope for a price list.

Sebalace
76 Main Street
Addingham
Ilkley
West Yorkshire LS29 0PL
England

A. Sells
'Lane Core'
49 Pedley Lane
Clifton
Shefford
Beds.
England

The particular materials used in this book are catalogued with details of suppliers on the following pages. The first column of addresses is for a postal service and the second for personal shoppers.

	Postal service	Personal shoppers
SHUTTLES		
Aero and Milward	*D.J. Hornsby* *Sebalace* *A. Sells*	Craft and wool shops Department stores
Handmade, wooden	*C. & D. Springett* 21 Hillmorton Road Rugby Warwickshire CV22 5BE England	
THREADS		
Coats threads	*Sebalace*	Craft and wool shops Details of local suppliers from: *J. & P. Coats* Marketing Services Dept National Distribution Centre 39 Durham Street Glasgow G41 1BS Scotland
DMC threads	*Larkfield Crafts* 4 Island Cottages Mapledurwell Basingstoke Hants England	Craft and wool shops Details of local suppliers from: *Dunlicraft Ltd* Pullman Road Wigston Leicester LE8 2DY England
HANDKERCHIEFS AND LINEN		
	D.J. Hornsby *Sebalace* *A. Sells*	Haberdashers
BEADS AND JEWELLERY FINDINGS		
	Creative Beadcraft Ltd Unit 26 Chiltern Trading Estate Earl Howe Road Holmer Green High Wycombe Bucks. England	*Ells and Farrier Ltd* 5 Princes Street Hanover Square London W1 England

	Postal service	Personal shoppers
WHEEL SEQUINS		
		Craft and wool shops Department stores
PAPERWEIGHTS		
	H. Thorn and Son 118–19 Fore Street Exeter EX4 3JQ England (discounts for quantity) *D.J. Hornsby* *Sebalace* *Dryad* *A. Sells*	*H. Thorn and Son*
VELOUR FABLON/STICKY BACKED FELT		
	D.J. Hornsby *Larkfield Crafts*	Hardware and DIY sh
DRIED LAVENDER		
	Sebalace	Craft shops Department stores
LACE MOUNTS		
Trinket boxes Handbag mirrors Bow brooches	*Framecraft Miniatures Ltd* 262 Rocky Lane Great Barr Birmingham B42 1QX England *Doreen Campbell* Highcliff Bremilham Road Malmesbury Wiltshire SN16 0OQ England *A. Sells*	

	Postal service	Personal shoppers
CRAFTACARD, BLANK CARDS AND ENVELOPES		
	Framecraft Miniatures Ltd	Art shops and stationers
SHEET CARD, SAFETY RULES, CRAFT KNIVES		
	Dryad	Art shops and stationers
GLUES		
Uhu		Stationers
Elmers School Glue	*Dryad*	Toy shops and stationers
CURTAIN RINGS		
		Hardware and DIY shops

Bibliography

Attenborough, Bessie M., *The Craft of Tatting*, Bell and Hyman, 1972.

Auld, Rhoda L., *Tatting*, David and Charles, 1974.

Hoare, Katherine L., *The Art of Tatting* (first published 1910), Lacis Publications, 1982.

Jones, Rebecca, *The Complete Book of Tatting*, Dryad Press, 1985.

Konior, Mary, *A Pattern Book of Tatting*, Dryad Press, 1985.

Nicholls, Elgiva, *Tatting*, Vista Books, 1962.

Nicholls, Elgiva, *Tatting Techniques*, Mills and Boon, 1976.

The Priscilla Tatting Book No. 2 (first published by the Priscilla Publishing Co., 1915), republished by Dover Publications, 1977, as Julia E. Sanders, *Tatting Patterns*.

Index